PICTURE
YOUR
PROSPERITY

PICTURE YOUR PROSPERITY

Smart Money Moves to
Turn Your Vision into Reality

Ellen Rogin, CPA, CFP®
&
Lisa Kueng

Portfolio / Penguin

PORTFOLIO / PENGUIN
Published by the Penguin Group
Penguin Group (USA) LLC
375 Hudson Street
New York, New York 10014

USA | Canada | UK | Ireland | Australia | New Zealand | India | South Africa | China
penguin.com
A Penguin Random House Company

First published by Portfolio / Penguin, a member of Penguin Group (USA) LLC, 2015

LIBRARY OF CONGRESS CATALOGING-IN-PUBLICATION DATA
Rogin, Ellen.
Picture your prosperity : smart money moves to turn your vision
into reality / Ellen Rogin, CPA, CFP, Lisa Kueng.
pages cm
Includes bibliographical references and index.
ISBN 978-1-59184-739-7
1. Finance, Personal. 2. Women—Finance, Personal. 3. Investments. I. Kueng, Lisa. II. Title.
HG179.R624 2015
332.024—dc23
2014038636

Printed in the United States of America
1 3 5 7 9 10 8 6 4 2

Set in Aldus LT Std
Designed by Alissa Rose Theodor

This publication is designed to provide accurate and authoritative information in regard to the subject matter covered. It is sold with the understanding that the publisher is not engaged in rendering legal, accounting, or other professional services. If you require legal advice or other expert assistance, you should seek the services of a competent professional.

While the author has made every effort to provide accurate telephone numbers, Internet addresses, and other contact information at the time of publication, neither the publisher nor the author assumes any responsibility for errors or for changes that occur after publication. Further, publisher does not have any control over and does not assume any responsibility for author or third-party Web sites or their content.

Our greatest hope for this book is that it will inspire women everywhere to make a difference in their own financial lives and in the lives of others. We would like to dedicate it to the two women who inspire us most—our moms.

To my mom, Chernie Shayman:
Thank you for teaching me about love, positivity, productivity, and baking! I miss you every day.

And to my mom, Therese Kueng:
Thank you for giving me faith in God, love to share, and wings to fly.

—Ellen and Lisa

CONTENTS

Introduction   1

Chapter One

Step One: Create Your Personal Vision   11

Chapter Two

Step Two: Take Charge of Your Financial Wellness   45

Chapter Three

Step Three: Design a Winning Plan   77

Chapter Four

Step Four: Make It Happen   113

Chapter Five

Step Five: Boost Your Financial
Happiness Quotient   157

Chapter Six

Step Six: Become Financially Resilient   183

Chapter Seven

Step Seven: Build a Lifetime of Prosperity   227

Acknowledgments   253

Notes   257

Index   265

IMPORTANT DISCLOSURES

The information contained in this book should not be construed as personalized investment advice, and should not be considered as a solicitation to buy or sell any security or engage in a particular investment strategy.

The opinions expressed in this book are those of the authors only and there is no guarantee that the views and opinions expressed in this book will succeed. No investment or financial planning strategy can assure success or protect against loss in declining markets. The strategies and concepts articulated in this book are for educational and illustrative purposes only and are not intended to provide financial, legal, or tax advice. Individuals are encouraged to seek professional guidance concerning their own unique situation.

The stories shared within this book are based on real situations. However, the names have been changed to protect the individuals' identity and the facts may have been altered to better demonstrate the particular message being conveyed.

Introduction

What does prosperity mean to you? Close your eyes for a moment and think about what comes to mind.

We've conducted hundreds of Prosperity Picture workshops across the country based on the ideas in this book, and that's always the first question we ask of our participants. It's a fascinating one because it results in a full spectrum of answers. Some people immediately say that, to them, prosperity means security or peace. Some say it means having time to do the things they find most rewarding. Some associate it with having money or being able to buy whatever they want. And some connect it with something very specific and seemingly unrelated, like "the ocean."

Merriam-Webster defines prosperity as "the condition of being successful or thriving; especially: economic well-being." So it's a word that refers to money, but it also refers to the rest of life. And it's true. The answers we hear when we ask, "What does prosperity mean to you?" fall into both of those categories—some are about money and some are about life. We love that! Your money is important, of course, but let's face it: money is meaningless if it can't be connected to the rest of your life. Who cares what the totals on your balance sheet or in your bank account are if you can't use them to build the kind of life you want? What good is having a brilliant investment strategy if you worry incessantly about losing it, constantly fight with your partner about money, or come home and kick your dog on days the market drops?

What if instead you felt positive, peaceful, and prosperous?

Most people see the logic in the fact that our money and our lives are inextricably linked, but ironically that doesn't necessarily lead them to think about their money as the exciting, potentially life-changing tool that it is. More often than not, we see people who think of their money as being contained in a silo—relegated to a special area they see as a necessary but separate part of life. They view their money silo in a variety of ways—sometimes it's a source of pain because there's not enough in it and sometimes it's a source of pain because there's too much in it. Some people are afraid of losing it, some can't wait to spend it all, and so on and so forth. Regardless of the specifics, most people tend to view their silo as something needing to be managed, but which is not intuitively linked with the rest of their life.

But what if we look at money differently? Not as a project that needs to be managed or an obstacle that needs to be overcome—and certainly not just a means to help us "get more stuff" or add to a collection of belongings. Instead, what could happen if we all began to view money as an incredible tool? A way to help us get closer each and every day to living the most extraordinary lives we possibly can, and also a tool we can use to help other people do the exact same thing? We see awakening to this possibility as incredibly exciting and inspiring. And so we've written this book as a way to help you define your personal version of true prosperity and to share ideas and direction on smart money moves you can make to turn that vision into reality.

As you begin reading, it will probably be fairly clear this book was written with women in mind. However, in the same way that we hope men will read magazine articles on "How to Keep Your Relationship Steamy," "How to Throw the Perfect Summer

Soiree," or even "Fourteen Days to a Perfectly Flat Stomach," we hope they will read this too. Even though the concepts are gender-neutral and apply to everyone, we have targeted them for women. We did this because as we look around we see women everywhere stepping into their fiscal power. Globally, women direct $20 trillion of purchases. They control more than half of the wealth in the United States. Women are earning more bachelor's and master's degrees than men. They comprise more than half of the U.S. work-force. And as women ourselves who have made our careers in the financial services industry, we wanted to build on this momentum and create a book that we hope will uniquely inspire women to create their own personal prosperity, use their money as a force for good in the world, and change the face of finances. This is *our* picture of true prosperity.

One of the first steps in this "Kumbaya" vision of women working to make the world better is to be a rock star in managing your own personal finances. You can't have a flourishing garden without first preparing your own soil and planting good seeds. We'll give you ideas on how to put clarity, meaning, and oomph into creating the life you want and the money moves you can make to help you get there. We have a warning, though: if you're looking for an exhaustive reference guide to money management, you've picked up the wrong book. Deep analysis obviously has an important place in financial planning, but we think it's best left for the number crunchers and "money geeks" of the world. In the same way you could improve your cholesterol levels without reading fifty pages about organic molecules and lipids, we believe there's a way to take control of your money without its having to be a snooze-fest that puts you to sleep even after your third cup of coffee. And while we're on the subject, we also believe it's possible for you to motivate yourself to improve your financial life without having to feel guilty you haven't done a better job of it in the past, ashamed about your saving habits, or worried you're a bad person because you spent money on a vacation last month. Your financial resources are the fuel to set your life in motion and we aim to show you how to make those resources sustainable and renewable—and to have a good time while you're doing it.

We won't be telling you how to outsmart the market or get rich quick by trading stocks out of your garage. This book contains no "hot stock tips." Please don't misunderstand; we've included lots of practical information on the building blocks you'll need to have a successful financial life and create your own prosperity. We provide you with detailed guidelines on how to create spending and savings plans that are right for you, how to make sure you have the proper insurance and estate plan intact, how to make sense of investing options and risk, and much more. If you read and put the basic precepts of this book to work for yourself, you will have done something that most people never do.

We've included all of this, and we've focused on what we believe are the most important points for you to know. The fact is, we don't think that advice on outsmarting the market or hot stock tips are particularly important for most people. And though they must be out there somewhere, we can't think of even one person we know who actually got rich trading stocks out of their garage. Comprehensive reference and technical books certainly serve an important purpose, but even we find them boring, so here we've cherry-picked the essentials for you.

This book is a canvas for you to create your personal picture of prosperity. It's a tool kit full of ideas you can use to bring your picture to life. It's a motivator to get out there and actually use those tools. It's a string around your finger to remind you of what you can be happy about. It's a stress ball you can pull out at those times when the thought of money brings nothing but anxiety. And you might even find it to be a kaleidoscope that can open up new ways of looking at what money and prosperity can mean in your life and in the world.

Tamara Chaponot is a wonderful example of someone who turned her vision of prosperity into reality. Tamara is a warm, vibrant, successful fashion retailer living in New York. She comes across in such a self-assured manner it's tempting to assume life as a fashionista has been easy for her. But that assumption, as is so often the case, is wrong. Tamara was born in the 1970s with a birth defect affecting her leg, and faced a serious risk as a child that she might never be able to walk. She underwent thirteen surgeries between the ages of two and eighteen, each of which required a hospital stay of about three months. That's a total of more than three years that she spent in the hospital. This kind of adversity, combined with the uncertainty of the outcome, might be enough to topple the spirit of most adults—never mind a child—but Tamara isn't most people!

During her hospital stays, Tamara began to "picture" things as a way of keeping her spirits up. One of the things she craved most was to be just like other kids and to feel "normal," so she pictured herself wearing stylish clothing instead of a hospital gown. She pictured herself looking "cool." She pictured her leg and the orthopedic shoes she had to wear covered up with circa 1975 bell-bottom jeans. As she continued to do this, fashion became more and more of a lifeline to her, and when she was able to return home between surgeries, she began plastering her bedroom walls with photos of beautiful clothing and models on fashion shoots that she snipped from magazines.

When she was around twelve years old, Tamara pushed her vision further and realized that when she was older she might be able to parlay her love of fashion into a business. She began to picture herself owning her own boutique, surrounded by the clothing she loved so much and earning enough money to make a nice life for herself. It was around that time her doctor at Shriners Hospital for Children in Chicago asked her to begin picturing something else as well. He asked Tamara to spend some time each day visualizing the healthy cells in her leg destroying the diseased cells. He compared the process to the game Pac-Man: "Picture the healthy cells munching away the sick cells, just like when you play Pac-Man," he told her. And so she began to picture this as well.

Over the next few years, Tamara's health began to improve. Whatever combination of surgery, ongoing medical care, and Pac-Man-style visualization was going on, something was working—Tamara was able to make a full recovery! There she was at age eighteen with her health restored, her bedroom walls covered with pictures of fashionable clothing, and her vision of a successful retail business firmly rooted in her mind. As you might guess, Tamara isn't the sort of person who lets a lot of grass grow under her feet. So she immediately got a series of jobs working in Chicago clothing boutiques as she started researching the fashion industry, reading books about how to run a successful business, and eventually writing a business plan. At age twenty-five she opened Clever Alice on Clark Street in Chicago, a shop targeting stylish twentysomethings who wanted unusual pieces and European flair at prices they could afford. In short order, musician Liz Phair became a Clever Alice client, *Lucky* magazine wrote a story about the shop, and Tamara began getting media attention as one of Chicago's youngest shop owners.

Several years later, after Tamara's business had been well established and she was enjoying life as an upwardly mobile young urbanite, she began to feel that something was missing. She didn't, on a conscious level, want to get married or have kids, primarily because she was afraid she might pass along a genetic predisposition to a birth defect to her children. But something was nagging at her, making her unhappy. So she asked herself, "Well, then, what does happiness look like?" Once again, she began picturing things. This time, instead of mink coats and mohair sweaters, her picture was of a man—a tall man—and . . . two kids! She wasn't even quite sure what the picture meant to her. But very shortly thereafter, when she was in the enviable position of having to fly home from a prêt-à-porter show in Paris, she noticed a French businessman staring across the plane aisle at her. As she caught his eye, he announced he was certain he knew her. It turned out he had been at the same show as she had, and the rest, as they say, is history. A year later the two were married at Chicago's city hall. Tamara eventually learned her birth defect was not genetic, so she didn't need to worry about passing it along to her own children. Today Tamara and her husband have two beautiful children and divide their time between New York and Paris. Tamara has evolved Clever Alice from a brick-and-mortar shop in Chicago to a series of retail pop-ups in Chicago and New York. She has an almost constant ear-to-ear smile on her face and, true to her childhood vision, she always looks "cool"!

How did this amazing series of events happen? If you ask Tamara, she'll say visualization has played a major role in getting her to the point in life she's at now. Can she prove her success was directly caused by those hours she spent in hospital beds picturing becoming a successful fashion retailer and willing the healthy cells in her leg to eat up the unhealthy ones, or picturing herself marrying her international-man-of-mystery husband and having children? Nope. Does she believe it was? Absolutely. And is there scientific support for the fact that her visualization could have contributed to the probability that these things would happen? Yes, there is—we'll tell you all about it in Chapter One.

In Tamara's story, it wasn't just visualization that made an impact. She thinks gratitude has also played a major role in her success. During her stays at the children's hospital, she observed lots of really difficult things: children with terminal cancer, kids who had been badly burned in horrible accidents, others battling serious physical disabilities with no chance of recovery. And even as a child she understood that her situation, though very difficult, could have been a lot worse. As a result, Tamara developed a practice of gratitude she continues to maintain. She regularly thinks through all she's thankful for, writes gratitude lists, and focuses on what's good in her life. We'll explore the amazing effects gratitude can have on our money and on our lives in this book.

Tamara is also a believer in giving. When Clever Alice had a brick-and-mortar presence and an ongoing inventory, she was regularly approached to donate items for silent auctions and other charitable initiatives and made it a point to give something to everyone who asked her. Now, as a mom to her two school-age children, she's committed to doing regular volunteer work at her kids' school. Giving—whether of your time, talent, or money—is another important component of prosperity that we'll discuss.

But most of all, if you ask Tamara how she got from being a hospital patient to being a wife, mother, and successful retailer, she'll say, "I trusted that it would work out." Tamara's story inspires us. Yet it doesn't inspire us because it's about someone who overcame an illness to create a fabulous life in fashion and a family that appears to have stepped off the pages of a glossy magazine. She could have overcome another type of adversity or had no adversity at all. Her story could just as easily be about becoming a doctor, a bartender, or a stay-at-home mom. She could be single or divorced, straight or gay, and have no kids or ten kids. None of those specifics are the reasons we find it inspiring.

We find it inspiring because it's a story of someone who proactively created her personal version of prosperity and trusted that things would work out. Not only that, but she accomplished a lot of this work as a child, using a combination of tools and techniques she hadn't been taught and couldn't possibly have known had a basis in science. Rather, she discovered them organically, trusting her gut and listening to herself the whole way through.

You may be saying to yourself, "Okay, Tamara pictured these things and it worked out well for her. But what does this have to do with money, investing, and reaching long-term goals?" Our answer for you? Everything.

This book is chock-full of the same kinds of tools and techniques that Tamara stumbled upon to create her version of prosperity and an extraordinary life. We've laid them out for you with easy-to-follow steps, fun and engaging activities, and research and scientific explanations to shed light on how and why they work. Visualization, gratitude, and giving are three powerful tools you can use to build your own prosperity. In addition, you'll learn other practical techniques you can use to take stock of where you stand financially and how to design a financial plan that can help move your ideas from a glimmer in your eye to reality. We'll also spend some time talking about how you can boost your financial happiness levels and develop your financial resilience. This is critically important—it's hard to feel prosperous when you're chugging

Pepto-Bismol out of the bottle because you're worried about the stock market crashing. And we'll end with some thoughts on how you can build a lifetime of prosperity for yourself and for others.

It begins and ends with you. Let's get started on creating your personal Prosperity Picture and exploring how you can make the smart money moves that can turn your vision into reality!

Chapter One

Step One:
Create Your Personal Vision

Have you ever imagined what you would do if you won a $100 million jackpot? Whether from lottery winnings, the slots in Vegas, or an inheritance from a long-lost aunt, what would you do with this sudden wealth? Maybe you don't think of one day having an influx of money but you daydream about the business you would love to start, or a beautiful home on the beach, or just having more time to practice yoga.

Most of us have been taught that daydreaming is a big, fat waste of time. But is it really? Could deliberate imagining possibly be the basis of a sound financial strategy? We've seen evidence again and again that having a clear personal financial vision of where you want to go is an essential part of reaching your financial goals.

Eight years ago Ellen's friend Sue told her, "I'm not happy in my career and I want to be able to retire when I'm fifty-eight." At the time she made this pronouncement, Sue was fifty-four years old and didn't have enough assets to last even five years in retirement. Sue wanted to know what she would need to do to reach that goal. As a believer in the benefits of thinking big, though not having the faintest idea how her friend would actually reach this goal, Ellen helped her run the numbers to see what it would take. She came up with a number that seemed pretty unachievable even to the Pollyannas among us. Sue would need to save more than $320,000 per year for the next four years to be able to retire in four years and keep her standard of living. This was an impossible feat based upon her current salary, but Sue was clear on her goal and passionate about getting to retirement bliss sooner rather than later. The discussion ended with Sue's going off to see what she could do and Ellen wishing her well, but not at all sure how it could happen.

And then an interesting series of events took place. First, Sue got a small raise—not enough to make her plan a reality, but definitely enough to move her in the right direction. Next, both a very sad and a very happy thing happened. First, her mother passed away unexpectedly. Sue had not been counting on a big inheritance, and it certainly was never part of her plan, but she did indeed receive one. Shortly after her mom's passing, she met a terrific guy whom she married the following year. (Could it be true that it always happens when we're not looking?)

Both of these events had a huge impact on Sue's financial situation. Over the next five years, she was in a position where she could leave her job, which she did. However, much to her surprise, it was not to retire. Instead, she felt financially secure in a way that gave her the courage to branch out and move to a job that she ended up enjoying much more. At that moment, she could have achieved her goal of ringing the retirement victory bell if she had wanted to, but instead she found something that made her much happier.

When Sue established her original vision of changing her life so she could feel happier, she had no way of knowing that she would be able to reach it in the way that she did, but she trusted in the process of creating a clear picture of increased life satisfaction and believing in it. And it ultimately paid off.

When it comes to financial planning, most people understandably focus on the basics—a saving and investing strategy, tax planning, reducing debt, and the like. But a personal financial vision? That may initially sound about as necessary for financial success as a cocktail umbrella is for a mai tai. It's not something you're likely to read about in the *Wall Street Journal* or even something that the typical financial advisor talks about. And yet it has the power to transform your money and your life. Creating a tangible personal financial vision on paper—this is what we call a "Prosperity Picture"—is one of the smartest money moves you can make and one that most people miss. Plus it's just plain fun!

What Is a Prosperity Picture?

First, let's define it. A Prosperity Picture is a visual depiction of what you want out of your life, now and in the future. It's an amalgam of images, created by you, that represents what you want your life to look and feel like. It's meant to be both a dreamscape and a road map—a simple visual showing where you really want to go and how that might impact your finances. And as a bonus, it takes only about fifteen minutes to create.

Have you ever read *The Little Prince* by Antoine de Saint-Exupéry? Lots of people read it in high school, especially in French class. It's a deceptively simple little book containing a lot of really profound ideas. In it, the Little Prince makes this observation: "Grown-ups love figures. When you tell them that you have made a new friend, they never ask you any questions about essential matters. They never say to you, 'What does his voice sound like? What games does he love best? Does he collect butterflies?' Instead, they demand: 'How old is he? How many brothers does he have? How much does he weigh? How much money does his father make?' Only from these figures do they think they have learned anything about him."

Let's face it. As adults in a busy, demanding, heavily materialistic society, we easily get caught up in "figures" instead of what the Little Prince refers to as "essential matters," especially when it comes to financial planning. Take college planning, for example. Between Ellen and Lisa, we have four children and stepchildren already in college or heading there soon. If the subject of going to college comes up at the random dinner party, the most common reactions range from a combo of eyebrow raising/knowing nods to the clenching of various body parts and a full-on rant about the obscene increase in college tuition costs, the competition to get into good schools, and the fact that, on top of all that, it can be tough for new grads to find work in this job market. These observations are all true, of course. And it's important—critical, actually—to plan for these kinds of practicalities. But are they "essential" in the way the Little Prince means? Probably not.

Let's also be real, though. Most of us are not conditioned to have a Little Prince sort of discussion at a typical dinner party. We're not likely to muse about what college students will discover about themselves and the world as they study humanities, art history, physics, or other subjects they may not even know exist when they enter school. Few of us will talk about how, during their college career, students may meet lifelong friends who have a profound impact on who they become as people. Or that they might be lucky enough to study abroad and experience entirely new cultures and ways of life firsthand. Why? Because we're adults and we're conditioned to talk first about "figures." The "essentials"—the things that give college (or whatever it is that's on your radar screen) meaning, provide joy, and get you excited to get up in the morning—often get relegated to second or third position as we move through life. Left unchecked, we may not even think of them at all. This is the first big reason we believe having your own personal Prosperity Picture is so important: it helps you focus on "the essentials" in your life. To quote our friend the Little Prince once again, it will help you remind yourself of "what games you love best" and whether you "like to collect butterflies."

The second reason we believe having your own Prosperity Picture is so important is that it will help you fine-tune your vision of your own future. How can you possibly plan for your financial future if you aren't clear on what you want that future to be? So as you look ahead to your life, what would you like to see? What would you like to happen in the next three weeks? Three months? Three years? How about beyond that?

It's a fun thing to think about—a pleasure, really—that most of us unfortunately don't often allow ourselves. Your Prosperity Picture will help you hone your vision so that you can get closer to turning the life you've imagined into a reality.

How Your Prosperity Picture Can Help You Achieve Your Goals: The Power of Visualization

The "active ingredient" in any given Prosperity Picture is visualization. Perhaps you've seen some of the recent media coverage or books about the power of visualization. It's an exciting aspect of brain science. Dr. Srinivasan Pillay, the Harvard Medical School–educated author of *Your Brain and Business: The Neuroscience of Great Leaders*, points out, "It is now a well-known fact that we stimulate the same brain regions when we visualize an action as we do when we actually perform that same action." This means that when you visualize yourself raising your left hand, it stimulates the same part of your brain that you use when you actually do lift your left hand. When you visualize yourself painting a beautiful still life, you stimulate the same part of the brain you use when you actually paint the still life. And the same can be true of our financial lives—when we visualize achieving a financial goal, we stimulate the same part of our brain that we use to actually achieve that financial goal.

Athletes have understood this for a long time. In a well-known study, Russian scientists compared the physical versus mental training schedules of four groups of Olympic athletes. The athletes took different training approaches. Group One did 100 percent physical training with no mental training at all. Group Two did 75 percent physical training and 25 percent mental training. Group Three did 50 percent each of physical and mental training. And Group Four did 75 percent mental training and only 25 percent physical training. Which group do you think performed best during the Olympics? It's not a trick question—if you guessed Group Four, you're right! This group spent the majority of their time on psychological preparation and envisioning themselves winning rather than on physical training, and they performed the best during the games. Of course, as Olympic athletes, they were obviously world-class talents in tip-top shape, which would certainly influence their performance. But so were the other athletes who spent more time on physical training. The implications are huge: visualization and mental preparation are powerful influences on success! This has been such an important finding that the U.S. Olympic Committee now has increased the number of full-time psychologists on staff from just one to six over the last twenty years.

Visualization is so powerful that it can even play a role in medical situations. Maureen, who was a baby nurse in Seattle in the 1970s, talks about visualization making a big impact in the delivery of babies. "We would routinely coach women giving birth to visualize peaceful places which make them feel calm and happy to help them get through the pain of childbirth," she says. She and her colleagues also coached mothers in the delivery room to focus on the specific physical changes they wanted their body to make throughout their labor, to picture the baby actually moving, and to emphasize other tangible details. "Using these visualization techniques made a huge positive difference for about 80 percent of the women I worked with," says Maureen. "The more people open themselves to the possibility that it can help, the better it works."

Similarly, Gina, a vivacious personal trainer in Denver, has a story of using visualization to help her overcome a physical obstacle. Gina was born with flat feet, which can be crippling. The problem had caused Gina pain for most of her life, but for the most part she had been able to manage it with physical therapy, special shoes, and other techniques. However, when she reached her late forties, the condition worsened considerably, affecting not just her feet but also surrounding muscles, and Gina could barely walk. Her prognosis wasn't good.

It was at that point that she began working with a well-known doctor who specializes in sports injuries using both a unique therapy technique called "dry needling" and also specific visualization. The first thing he did was tell Gina that he himself "does not believe in flat feet." (Remember that when you get to our discussion of the power of beliefs in Chapter Four.) Next he asked her whether she was willing to put aside all of the negative things she had been telling herself and all of the things she had learned about her problem, and to look at the situation differently. He coached her to visualize her feet having arches, to visualize herself walking and running, and to picture herself feeling well and being healed. Something about the combination of her doctor's physical technique, her own visualization, and the positive thinking began to work. Within two years, she was walking again, and at a recent fitness boot camp was asked to take center stage and lead eight thousand people in a series of warm-up exercises to start their day. "That was such a high point for me," she explains. "I went from being unable to walk to being able to lead a huge physical fitness initiative . . . I'm a walking, talking miracle!"

And here's the thing: each and every one of us can apply these visualization and mental preparation techniques to our financial situations in the same way athletes, mothers in labor, and patients apply them. How do you visualize your future? What do you want to see happen and what resources will you need to pay for it? What moves will you make to be financially successful? Based upon our many collective years in financial services, we know this is not a typical approach. The financial services industry tends to focus more on facts, figures, and whether you're satisfied with your on-line bill-paying service than it does on helping you visualize financial success. But trust us—it works, and it works very effectively. Here's the science behind it.

How Does Visualization Work?

Brain science says the reason visualization works is due in part to a small area of our brains—just about the size of your little finger—located at the base of our brain stems. This is the reticular activating system, or RAS, and its job is to filter incoming information and decide how important it is. Think of the last time you went from your home to a place you routinely go, like the office or a friend's house. How much did you pass that you did *not* notice? Probably most of it, right? You couldn't focus on it all because if you did you probably never would have made it there! It would have been completely overwhelming, so your RAS had to prioritize what was most important for the task at hand and filter everything else out.

Let's look at an example of information the RAS allows in. Do you have a recent memory of buying a car? What make, model, and color was it? After you bought it, how many cars of that exact make, model, and color did you start noticing on the street? If you're like most people, you started seeing "your" car all over the place. If you've experienced this phenomenon, do you think it's because all of a sudden more of those cars were being manufactured? Probably not. It's because after you bought yours, it took on significance it didn't have before and therefore made its way onto your subconscious "radar screen." It's not as though you left your house each morning thinking "Today I'm going to go out and look for every black Volkswagen Jetta I can find," but you saw the cars anyway. That's your RAS at work—separating information it deems relevant for you from information that it doesn't on a subconscious level. It doesn't take much extrapolation to see the huge role that the RAS plays for all of us. It's the part of our brain that quite literally sees things or doesn't, that hears things or doesn't, that registers opportunity or misses it, that makes us consciously aware of options or keeps those options hidden from our conscious awareness. Think of the RAS as your brain's gatekeeper.

Brain Training and Goals

Now here's the really exciting part—you can help set the filter on your RAS. As you know, the brain is a muscle, and just as you might condition other muscles like biceps, you can also condition your brain. The point of conditioning your RAS is to help it screen for information you can use to get closer to achieving your goals and move that information into the active part of your brain. The conditioning is simple—it begins by clearly establishing what you want to happen. You can do this by writing down your goals, creating actual pictures of them, or visualizing them in detail. Once you've established your goals, the next step is to maintain an ongoing focus on them. These simple techniques help your brain know what to look out for. Without the conditioning, critical information that can help you achieve your goals might remain background noise. We are all governed by our RAS—it functions without our conscious thought, much as our lungs pump air without our having to think about doing it. But just as we can influence and maximize the benefits of our breathing if we think about it, we can influence and maximize the benefits of our RAS by thinking about it. Said another way, we all listen to our RAS (we don't have a choice), but very few of us talk to it.

We've heard lots of inspiring stories of people "talking" to their RAS. More than a decade ago, Lisa's dear friend Melissa was at a career impasse. She had a law degree but didn't want to practice in a corporate environment, so she decided to talk to her RAS by writing her career goals on index cards. She wrote that she wanted to practice law in a nurturing environment, earn a certain salary, and work with people she could truly enjoy. She then began her new job search, reviewing and contemplating her index cards on a regular basis as she went along. Within a couple of months she got an offer to work for the Illinois state court system that met most of her written goals but not quite all of them. Nonetheless, she took it and put her index cards away in a desk drawer. About two years later, when she ran across the cards long forgotten in the back of her drawer, she realized that by that point each and every one of her criteria had been met! Conditioning the RAS can be a powerful thing.

Margaret in New Jersey credits talking to her RAS through visualization as being the primary factor in her being able to attend her college of choice and later, after she married, as being instrumental in helping her advise and support her husband in overcoming multiple obstacles to build a successful military career. "You have to leave your mind and your heart open to possibilities and you can't close that inner door," she says. "That will allow the opportunity to flow through."

Focusing your RAS in this manner can also help you to establish and "speak your goals out loud." After doing visualization exercises in a workshop in South Carolina, one woman shared with a group of forty-five people that she had a dream of quitting her current job and opening a bed-and-breakfast. Next, two others shared their goal of starting a shelter for women who are victims of domestic abuse. Not bad for one night! In another workshop, a recently widowed and still very heartbroken woman of seventy-five realized she would like to go on a bus tour vacation with one of her lady friends. She had the means to take the trip, and though this was a relatively simple thing for her to do, she hadn't been emotionally ready to acknowledge it before that night. She left with tears of courage in her eyes, hugging people she had met only that evening. These inspiring, motivational moments may sound like they're made for TV, but they're real.

Goal setting doesn't always have to be "made for TV." If we dip back into a more pedestrian reality for a moment, most of us also want things from our lives that may not be quite as . . . extraordinary. One woman at a workshop simply wanted the opportunity to regularly go someplace by herself where she could have peace and quiet and be completely alone. It didn't have to be elaborate—a weekly trip on her own to the public library would be perfectly fine with her. Another wanted to travel with her husband during retirement. Many have goals of simply feeling secure, being healthy, and having time to enjoy their friends.

Though vastly different people with a wide spectrum of goals, all of those individuals shared one thing in common: they increased their chances of making their dreams and goals actually happen by conditioning their RAS to look for opportunities and options that might help them along the path. In a few moments, you'll have the chance to do the same thing.

Creating Your Prosperity Picture, Part One: Conditioning Your RAS

So let's get started with conditioning your RAS right now. It sounds like a really big deal, doesn't it? Perhaps like something you might need to get a doctor's permission to do? Well, it *is* big, because it has profound implications, but it's not complex at all. No physician's approval is required and you don't need to take a day off work to do it. It's really quite simple—it's a matter of exploring and clarifying your own vision for the future. And it begins with identifying what your goals are. This can be a big question, right? We've all had experiences when, upon being asked what our life goals are or where we want to be in five years, our reaction has been less a comprehensive, insightful review of what's most important in our lives and something more like "I'm not even sure what I'm going to have for dinner—how the hell should I know what my life goals are?"

Lisa was once chatting with her friend Jackie and asked whether she had made it to a concert they had discussed. In a resigned, somewhat disappointed tone, Jackie said, "No . . . I stayed home to work on my life plan." It's certainly impressive that Jackie worked on such a thing (because, let's face it, most people don't), but her tone suggested something less than positive. It was as if she had announced she stayed home to clean out her gutters with a toothbrush. But it's also understandable. It can seem like hard work and easily raise a lot of big, overwhelming questions. But this approach will be both fun and easy. We promise. Part of the reason is that we're going to help you take a shortcut into your psyche by beginning with some pictures.

In the center of this book you'll find a set of images that we ask you now to remove. If you prefer to keep the book's images intact, go to the PictureYourProsperity.com Web site and find the Book Bonuses tab. When prompted, type in the password "PYPnow" and you'll be able to access the same photos, which you can print out. You'll also need a pair of scissors and a notebook to use for this first activity and throughout the book—we will refer to this as your Prosperity Notebook. It can be one of those lovely clothbound journals, a spiral notebook from the drugstore, or, frankly, even a sheaf of scrap paper that you staple or clip together. These are the raw materials you'll work with to condition your RAS.

First, remove the images from this book or gather those you've printed from the Web site. Next, cut them apart so that the images are separated. Now lay them out so you can see them all at once and take a look. Which ones resonate with you? They might represent something you want to have more of now or something you want to create for the future. Separate the ones that appeal to you most— as many as you want. You don't have to know why they appeal to you, and you don't have to know how you'll achieve them. If you like 'em, pick 'em—easy as that.

Next, take a look at what you've chosen and identify between one and three images that really speak to you. Don't place too much significance on this choice. We're not asking you to define yourself by these selections, nor are we saying these are the only images you'll ever like, just that they resonate with you and, at least for the moment, they stand out more than the others. Now pick just one to focus on—any one. This is the one we would like you to use for your first RAS-stimulating visualization exercise. (You can go back to the others later.) The exercise has two parts. First we'll ask you to work through all the questions by just thinking about them. Then we'll ask you to write your answers down. When you're ready, put your selected image in front of you and have a pen and your Prosperity Notebook handy for when the visualization is complete. Make sure you are in a quiet, comfortable place where you will be undisturbed for the next few minutes. You can do this with your eyes open or closed. We prefer eyes closed, but do whichever is more comfortable for you.

Ready?

• Begin by taking in a few deep breaths. Inhale through your nose and exhale through your mouth. With each inhale feel more and more relaxed, and with each exhale feel more calm and peace. If any distracting thoughts come up, just put them aside for now; you can come back to them later. As you bring the image to your mind, what does it represent to you? What specific goal does it inspire? One of Lisa's favorite images is the mountain scene with flowers. To her, it represents the view of her and her husband's patio at a villa in Tuscany, which they visualize themselves renting in retirement. To other people that same image represents traveling in Colorado, a general suggestion of peace and serenity, the ability to enjoy a healthy outdoorsy lifestyle. There is, of course, no "correct" answer or interpretation—the only thing that matters is what you think. We'll all see and feel exactly what we need to as we look at these images. Remember, don't worry about logistics—you don't need to know how you're going to pay for it, when you'll find the time to do it, or how it will work. Just enjoy it! There is no hurry. Take as long as you need to understand what this image represents to you.

• Let's get more specific. If the idea you're visualizing does not already have a physical location associated with it, imagine what the location might be, just as if you were filming a movie and needed a movie set. Picture your vision in your mind's eye as if it were happening now, in the present moment.

• This next part is especially powerful. Imagine you're there now observing yourself—sort of like you're now watching the movie and it's featuring you as the star. This is a chance to think about details like what you're doing and how you look. In this part, you might imagine yourself scampering on the beach in a flowing sundress, outfitted head to toe in outdoorsy gear as you captain a sailboat, or wearing huge sunglasses and sitting on a veranda in Portofino. That's the fun of this—you get to decide! Who else is in your movie? Are you alone or are there other people with you? If there are others there, are they talking and interacting? What are they saying? What are you saying?

• Now let's explore your senses. What does the air feel like around you? What sounds do you hear in the background? The ocean? Music? Street noise? How about smells? Smells can be so evocative— what do you smell in the air? In Tahiti, we might smell salt air, suntan lotion, or fresh coconut. Perhaps you smell your favorite foods cooking on the stove top, scented candles in your living room, fresh baked bread on the streets of Paris. Open all of your senses and fully immerse yourself in your vision.

• This final part of the visualization is a chance to notice how you feel as your vision is happening. What emotions are you experiencing? Where in your body do you feel these emotions? Some experts theorize that your subconscious mind is unable to discern the difference between how you feel when you're actually experiencing something and how you feel when you just imagine that you're experiencing it. So emotionally and subconsciously, it may be just as powerful to feel joy at the thought of winning a first gold medal as it is to actually win it. That power is huge! How does the Olympian feel as she crosses the finish line? How does the painter feel when she completes her masterpiece? How does a mother feel as she watches her son receive his college diploma? The power of those emotions can turbocharge your plans and help transform your goals into reality in ways you're not even aware of. What are you feeling? Take time to linger and enjoy this vision and all it has to offer you.

• When you feel your vision is complete, gently open your eyes.

That completes the visualization portion of the exercise. Fun, huh? Now it's time to write down a few notes about what you just experienced. Your answers don't have to be long or detailed if you don't want them to be, but they do have to be written. This will help stimulate your RAS. Here are the main questions to ask yourself:

• What is the selected image?
• What specific goal does it inspire?
• Where specifically are you?
• What details do you see?
• Who is there with you (if anyone)?
• What are they saying?
• What do you hear in the background?
• What do you smell in the air?
• How do you feel?

Take a look at what you've written, and read it out loud. Allow yourself to spend a bit more time there. Are you enjoying the process? If you are, try it with another image, and keep going. Use these visualizing techniques for as many images as you'd like.

Creating Your Prosperity Picture, Part Two: Putting Your Goals Together

We're going to move on and give these images you chose a greater context by walking you through how you can quickly and easily create your personal Prosperity Picture. As we discussed earlier, your Prosperity Picture is a visual depiction of what you want out of your life, beginning *right now* and then moving into the future. As both a dreamscape and a road map, it will show where you really want to go and how that might impact your finances.

To create yours, you'll need a large sheet of sturdy paper or poster board (ideally eleven by seventeen inches or larger). This will become your Prosperity Picture Frame. Consider it a blank canvas. To move forward with this step, take a few minutes and gather the following items:

- The paper or cardboard for your Prosperity Picture Frame.
- A pen or marker.
- All of the images that you liked and selected in Part One. Also, if you have your own photos, magazine pictures, or other images that you would like to include, please do so. Feel free to use as many images as you want for this—no limits. (Also, you can discard the images you don't like— you won't need them.)
- Something adhesive—tape, glue, or paste.

Take your Prosperity Picture Frame and draw a line down the center of the frame and another line across the middle. You now have four large boxes. Along the left-hand side of your frame, write "More Money" at the top and "Less Money" at the bottom. Along the bottom of your frame, write "Sooner" on the left and "Later" on the right. (See the image on page 29 as a guide.) Since the left side of the frame says "Sooner" and the right side says "Later," the idea here is for you to arrange the images you chose based on when you might like to see them in your life. The left side

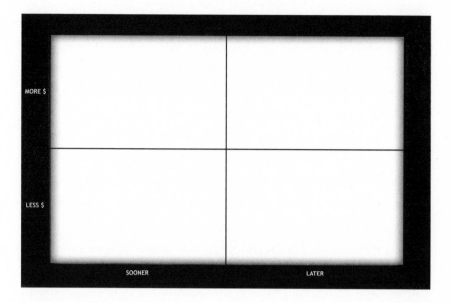

is for images representing goals you would like to accomplish soon—within the next five years, say. The right side is for goals you would like to accomplish later—five years or longer. Similarly, the bottom half of the frame, "Less Money," and the top, "More Money," are both guiding you to begin to think about how much the goals represented by each image might cost. If an item is relatively low cost (or even free), it belongs in the bottom half. If it represents more serious cash, it belongs in the top. All together, you have four boxes within the frame: "Sooner/Less Money," "Sooner/More Money," "Later/Less Money," and "Later/More Money."

Your next step is to place each image you like in one of the four boxes within the frame. For example, let's say you've chosen the image of the woman doing yoga. If you already know how to do yoga, it requires little to no money to do it, so it stays on the bottom half—"Less Money." And if you're a yoga person, you probably practice it now on a somewhat regular basis, so it falls on the left side—"Sooner."

The airplane image is also a popular one. For many people, it represents traveling during retirement. This is something that would obviously require money and, if you're not already retired, something that would take place later in life. So here we have a good example of the "Later/More Money" category.

You may find yourself wanting to place some images right smack in the middle of the frame. The volunteer image is a good example— if that image means volunteering at your local soup kitchen, it may not cost a dime. But if it means going to another country for a work trip that requires volunteers to pay their own way, it may represent a substantial cost. It could also easily represent both of those ideas to you, so placing it right in the middle of "Less Money" and "More Money" may make perfect sense. Likewise, some of the images such as health and friends could represent things you want to focus on in your life now and that you'll value later on as well—so they too might be placed right in the middle of "Sooner" and "Later." You should place each of your images wherever they feel right.

Remember, there are no conditions—don't worry about whether you'll *really* be able to do this or whether you'll have time or money for whatever the image represents to you. This is also an opportunity to add images to your Prosperity Picture. These may be actual photos or images from magazines or catalogs—whatever speaks to you. If you've always wanted to go bungee jumping in New Zealand or host your own TV show, then add images reflecting these goals.

Above all, remember that your Prosperity Picture is uniquely yours—there's no "right" way to create it. The time frame we suggested above is a general guide, but you can decide on what that means for you specifically. Some people are rooted in the present and near term—their "later" might mean six to ten years from now, and they can't or don't care to think much beyond that. Others are already talking about where they want to retire even though it's twenty-five years away. Not sure how far or broad you want to go with your Prosperity Picture? Listen to your gut. Look at the images in front of you and think about which ones get you most excited. Begin there and add as you go—let your intuition steer you.

Once you get the images close to where you want them, take a good look at them, make your final tweaks, and stick them down! Now, we know you'll probably resist actually sticking them down, perhaps because you're not sure they're exactly where you want them, but we encourage you to do it. You need to have a Prosperity Picture that is complete and intact so you can touch it, feel it, and hang it up somewhere prominent. If you use just a little bit of tape, you can always adjust your images later.

So go ahead and get started. Creating your Prosperity Picture can expand your thinking and get you to see your life in new ways. Enjoy it!

Exploring What Your Prosperity Picture Means

After your Prosperity Picture is complete, sit back and take a moment to enjoy what you've created. Soak it in. Take a few deep breaths, relax, and contemplate what the images mean to you individually and also collectively. When you're ready, grab your Prosperity Notebook and write down a few notes about your creation. We find this works best as a narrative. Write a description of what your Prosperity Picture means as though you're telling your story to a friend. Enjoy the process. Let yourself get lost in the details.

And remember, this is not a vague idea taking place at an unnamed point in the future. This is a description of you and your life—and it begins *right now*!

When we do workshops, this is always our favorite part. The excitement and energy level is through the roof, and we hear amazing stories of people's Prosperity Pictures. A smiling, sincere thirtysomething named Susan attended one of our workshops in New England. For her Prosperity Picture, she placed the friends photo and the image of the plant growing in the "Sooner/Less Money" box, and several photos that represented money and security in the "Sooner/More Money" box. Her "Later/More Money" section was full of images that reminded her of travel and leisure. And her "Later/Less Money" section was just two photos: one of the older couple holding hands and the volunteer image. Susan explained that she recently got divorced and was on the verge of bankruptcy because her ex-husband had racked up an overwhelming amount of debt in both of their names. Many people would have (understandably) been beaten down and embittered by such a situation. But not Susan. She was smiling from ear to ear almost the whole time she described her Picture to a room of thirty women. She explained she'd picked the friends image because she was grateful for her wonderful friends who were helping her get through this difficult time. She chose the plant photo because it reminded her she needed to nurture herself each day. She went on to say her most immediate goals were to get through her personal financial crisis, rebuild her credit, and find ways to earn, save, and invest extra money. Later on she might like to start dating again and find more time for volunteer work. And ultimately she would like to be in a position to travel, see the world, and enjoy herself, her family, and her friends. After the workshop that evening, she gave us a hug, grabbed her Prosperity

Picture, and walked off with her signature smile plastered on her face. A truly inspirational moment!

Susan's Picture can serve as a powerful tool to help her get out of debt and become financially secure. The more she visualizes her individual goals, the more her RAS will be alert to opportunities for her to move toward them. These moments of opportunity can range from "Hmm, Susan, maybe you can try this new recipe for dinner tonight—then you don't need to spend money on expensive takeout" to "Hey, isn't that Steve, the accountant from the dog park? Didn't he mention he had some ideas that could save you money on taxes?" The more Susan acts on these helpful impulses and begins to reap positive results, the better she'll feel and the more she'll be motivated to continue.

In addition to helping you clarify the essentials, focus on your goals, and condition your RAS, creating your own Prosperity Picture can help you make more strategic financial planning choices along the way. Lisa and her husband Tony have a retirement vision of downscaling their current home in Chicago and renting places for a month or two at a time in other cities where they can live and work—LA, San Francisco, even Florence or Rome. Recently, in the middle of refinancing their current mortgage, they discussed the advantage of making extra principal payments so their house could be paid off sooner (which, by the way, is a tactic that can save thousands of dollars in interest and turn mortgagees into owners much more quickly than it would otherwise take). As they dutifully started planning to take this approach, all of a sudden they looked at each other and said, "Wait a minute—our vision is to spend half the year in other places, and that's something we're aiming to do within the next eighteen to twenty years. This is a thirty-year mortgage. If we make extra payments, we may get the house paid off in twenty-two or twenty-five years instead of thirty, but we'll probably have sold it by then." For them, it made more sense to invest that extra money rather than put it into the house. Had they not laid out the vision for themselves, they probably would have made some financial decisions that, while sound in and of themselves, would not have helped them get closer to making their personal vision a reality.

There are as many Prosperity Picture stories as there are people. Sheila is an older woman who loves the arts and lives in the South. She's fortunate enough to have a very comfortable lifestyle and designed a Prosperity Picture focused on giving back and patronizing her local opera company. Laura, a woman living in a Midwest farming community who is struggling to make ends meet, created a Prosperity Picture focused mainly on pursuits requiring little or no money—spending time with friends, growing a low-cost kitchen garden, and exercising. Nicole, a mother of five in New Jersey, built her Prosperity Picture around the volunteer work she would like to do for a global literacy organization while also raising and supporting her children.

For you, of course, there's one Prosperity Picture that matters most and that's your own. So go ahead. If you haven't already done it, take a few minutes and write down the story of your Prosperity Picture. If you have done it, pull it out and take another look. What do your pictures say about you, your dreams, and your plans for right now and beyond? What juicy details can you add? This is your story—go for it!

You might notice some patterns on your Picture. Do you have a lot of images on the "Later" side of your board and relatively few on the "Sooner" side? If so, is it because you're doing all you want to do right now and you've got the most important things covered?

Or do your goals feel so big or unattainable that you don't think you can achieve them anytime soon? Could it be that you're putting off some of the things in life you find most rewarding? These may be profound questions for you, so give yourself some time to really think about them. If you're not satisfied with the answers you're coming up with, what can you do differently? What are you waiting for? What needs to happen for you to focus on doing more of what you want right now? After all, life is now, isn't it? On the other hand, if almost everything is on the "Sooner" side and you have few long-term goals visualized, consider what that means to you. Do you feel anxious about planning for the future? Concerned that you may not make it there? If that's the case, is it a source of anxiety for you? What implications does it have for the choices you're making now?

You can ask the same types of questions if most of your images are placed either above or below the "money line." If most of your images are in the "More Money" section, what does that say about your life right now? Is it difficult for you to appreciate the simpler things in life that don't necessarily require a lot of money? If so, are you okay with that? Conversely, if most everything you've chosen is in the "Less Money" category, why is that? Does your Picture genuinely reflect what you're after or could it mean you don't believe that goals representing more money are feasible, so you're not even going to try? Lisa was on a business trip in Miami with her coworker John when a luxury boat show was going on right across the street. John was fascinated by the boats, had checked them all out from afar, and was chatting about how much he would love to have one. Lisa asked if he had gone over to check them out and he laughed. "I'll never be able to own something like that," he said. "It's way beyond reality." Is it? Maybe. It's possible that he could start saving and investing with the goal of buying one of those luxury yachts and never make it. But if he never tries? Well, then of course he's almost sure never to make it.

If you find your images skewed in any of these directions, do yourself a favor. Take a few minutes and turn off your phone. Close the door. Take a few deep breaths, do some neck rolls, and unclench. Now close your eyes and think. What's going on, really? Why are your images clustered the way they are? What does the pattern mean to you? Is your viewpoint mostly positive or mostly negative? If it's mostly positive, great—you now have even greater clarity, and hopefully motivation for where you're going. If it's mostly negative, what can you do differently? How can you reframe some of these ideas and goals to feel better about them? What obstacles do you need to get past to feel better? And what can you do about those obstacles? To be clear, there is no right or wrong here, and you're the only one who knows the answer for you. This is simply an area to notice and pay attention to, and if you're truly open and honest with yourself, thinking about it may very well open up a useful path.

Creating Your Prosperity Picture, Part Three: Keeping Your Vision in Sight

You've now created something exciting and potentially life changing. Please don't put it in your sock drawer. We get that you probably won't display this above your sofa, but put it up somewhere where you can see it every day. Tack it onto a bulletin board, hang it on your closet door or on the fridge. This is important. It won't be nearly as helpful if it's in a drawer or the back of your closet—you need to be able to see it to keep that brain-imprinting process constantly working. If you travel frequently, take a "picture of your Picture" and carry it with you so you can see it while you're gone—if you have a smartphone, you can keep it right there.

As you pass by it, take a moment and think about it, at least once a day. You may not have time to think about it in its entirety, but get into the habit of picking out just one image and consciously focusing on what it means to you. Let's say you've hung your Prosperity Picture on the fridge, and one of your favorite photos is the couple hiking and looking at the waterfall. Maybe that means a trip to Hawaii with your significant other. As you're in the kitchen waiting for your bagel to toast, take a moment and think about that. Go there, just as you did earlier with the vision questions, except this time you don't need ten minutes, or a pen, or your Prosperity Notebook. You just need that moment. Close your eyes and picture the waterfall, envision the color of the rocks, the plants growing on shore, and the blue sky. Feel your partner's arm around your shoulders and the warmth of the sun on your face. Smell the fresh air. Feel the peace. Just for that moment. And then bring your attention back to your bagel that's just popped out of the toaster and get on with your day. What did you just do? At the simple end of the spectrum, you had a pleasant sensation that you wouldn't otherwise have had while you waited for your breakfast. At the complex end of the spectrum, you gave your RAS a workout and imprinted the idea that at some point you *will* be standing in Hawaii looking at that waterfall! The more you do that, the more your subconscious mind will help you figure out a way to get there, even if you're not aware of it.

Meg in Chicago has tacked her Prosperity Picture on the bulletin board above her desk and does visualization exercises with one particular photo almost every day—the airplane. For her it means a deluxe African safari that she will one day take. Desiree, a successful real estate broker, created a Prosperity Picture that includes the dinner and wine photo. For her it means a trip to Prague she plans to take with her mother and daughter. She visualizes it constantly and has actually begun to make travel plans.

Natalie, a seventysomething woman in Connecticut, has an amazing story of how this worked for her. When she was fresh out of college in the 1960s, she spotted a forest green Jaguar with a beautiful beige interior and the iconic silver animal on the hood— and fell in love with it. For her it was an "emblem of high society." Though she couldn't come close to affording it then, it made a big impression on her and the image imprinted solidly in her mind. Many years later, as she was starting up her own health care business, she ran across a photo of that exact car and decided it was a good symbol of making her new venture a success. So she cut it out and taped it on the wall of her closet where she would see it every day. About three years after she taped up the photo, Natalie's sister asked her to go out to help her shop for a new car. Natalie agreed, and in the middle of the shopping expedition she somewhat idly wandered off into the pre-owned section of the dealership. And there it was—"her" Jaguar! It was exactly as she'd remembered it when she first saw it in her twenties, and exactly like the one that had been taped to her closet wall for three years—forest green, beige interior, shiny animal on the hood! It was priced to sell, and without hesitation she bought it on the spot, drove it home, and sat on her front porch in the rain staring at it for an hour. After years of imprinting, Natalie had turned her vision into reality!

Coupled Up? Deepen Your Financial Intimacy by Creating a Shared Vision

We hope Natalie's story, and the stories of the many other women in this chapter, inspire you about the possibilities for your own future. Now let's take a look at how you can use the power of visualization with a significant other. If you have a spouse or partner, you can also use the techniques we've discussed in this chapter to enrich your relationship and create a shared vision of your future together. (If you don't have a spouse or partner, perhaps you would like to do some or all of these activities with a close friend or family member. If not, you can simply skip this section.)

Think of your partner. What do you want from the life you share? What do the two of you want to do together? Do you want to travel to Japan? Buy a sailboat? Start your own soup kitchen? It's funny, but life gets so busy for couples, especially if you have kids, that it's easy to focus only on the day-to-day responsibilities and never give yourselves time to dream and plan.

The best starting point for optimizing your financial lives as a couple is to think about your future together in the same way you did as an individual earlier in this chapter. Here are some simple, practical ideas for the two of you to jump-start the process:

If you've already selected the vision cards that appeal to you, get them now and lay them out. If you haven't, take the time to make your selections now.

To get an extra set of images for your partner, go to PictureYour Prosperity.com and find the Book Bonuses tab. When prompted, type in the password "PYPnow" and you'll be able to access the same photos we've included in this book. Print them out.

Pick a time when the two of you can sit down and spend at least thirty minutes or so without interruption. You may even want to make an event out of this: open up a nice bottle of wine, sit down in front of the fireplace, sit outside—whatever you like to do together. Most importantly though, give yourself permission to enjoy the experience.

Begin by asking your partner to do the same thing you've already done—select all the images he or she would like to see more of in life now or down the road.

Then read the visualization questions aloud and have your partner either write down the answers or answer them silently. If you haven't done this part yet yourself, you do it too. If you have, just take the time to recall your answers. Then share what you "saw." It's amazing what you may find. When Lisa did this with her husband Tony, he envisioned the two of them entertaining guests in their home, which is something they often do already, but this time it was in Los Angeles, not Chicago, where they currently live. In this vision, Tony was imagining that they lived part-time in LA and that new friends were included around the table—people who worked in the music industry, which is Tony's life pursuit. Lisa hadn't been at all aware that he was interested in living part-time in LA, and in fact neither had he until he did the vision exercise! Just think of the possibilities for you and your partner.

Next, ask your significant other to create his or her own Prosperity Picture, just as you did above. When you both have yours ready, spend some time describing your Pictures to each other—really tell your story, as we discussed earlier. Focus on what you've each created—this can be incredible stuff!

After you have this discussion, you may decide you would like to create a Couples Prosperity Picture, in which you decide what your combined goals, hopes, and dreams look like. Just print more images and sit down with a fresh "frame" and some tape.

Know that even if you don't create an actual combined Prosperity Picture, you can still use these conversations for fodder to have a rich discussion about your shared vision of the future. Make some notes in your Prosperity Notebook about what you want to do together. Or better yet, create a Couples Prosperity Notebook as a tool the two of you can keep coming back to. Having a shared vision of your lives and your money can help you build a strong financial relationship and create a forum for open communication, respect, and give-and-take. This is your life together—enjoy the process!

Speaking of enjoying the process, if you've tracked along with all of the suggestions in this chapter, you've accomplished a lot and hopefully had some fun along the way. At this point, you're officially done with this first foundational step of creating your own Prosperity Picture.

One point of clarification here: this is a mental-conditioning technique, not a pipe dream. We're not suggesting these images will magically appear in your life, or that you should use your Prosperity Picture as a birthday wish list or bridal shower registry. We're not saying that you can use this technique to "sign up" for the universe to bring you a lake house, a charitable foundation, or your own pony. What we know is this is a simple, repeatable, and fun process you can use to explore and clarify what you want your own future to hold, as well as one that will help condition your subconscious.

What's more is that this process is inextricably linked with your financial strategy. It may not be obvious, but in going through the visualization process, you've created the beginning of a powerful financial plan. You may already have a more traditional written financial plan, but if you're like most of us, it lacks this visual element, which has the potential to put it on steroids. If you don't have a written financial plan, you'll still need to add elements to make it complete, of course, but this is the first and most critical step, and many investors never do it. They open up accounts, they make investments, but they never take the time to clarify *why* they're doing it. You have just begun the process of clarifying where you're going. You've started to create your Prosperity Picture. In the following chapters we will give you tools to clarify, build, and enhance your future vision.

Gain Traction Through Action

- Make sure you have a Prosperity Notebook. You will be using this throughout the book to note your "aha" realizations, areas for follow-up, and inspired prosperity thoughts.
- Do the visualization exercise in this chapter with images that you're especially drawn to. Let yourself go there—it can be incredibly fun.
- Create your Prosperity Picture. Don't wait to do this powerful activity. Your own easy-bake Prosperity Picture with all the ingredients is right in this book!
- Spend time with your images and the Prosperity Picture as a whole reflecting on what they represent to you. Are there other images you want to add? Go ahead and add them.
- Hang your Picture in a place where you can see it every day. Spend a few moments each day looking at and visualizing the goals associated with those pictures.

- If you're part of a couple, turbocharge your financial relationship by doing the visualization exercise together and then each creating your own Prosperity Picture. Discuss your Pictures, and consider making a Couples Prosperity Picture.

Chapter Two

Step Two:
Take Charge of Your Financial Wellness

Our friend Jim has parents who had a dream for retirement. In fact they had the *classic* dream for retirement: they wanted to put their stuff in storage, buy an RV, and set out on the open road. The good news is, they did it—they finished their last official days of work, bought the RV, and set their dreams into motion. The bad news is that they hadn't really thought through the details. They were planning a relatively modest approach, no splurges or luxurious activities, so they reasoned their social security income would cover their basic expenses. But there were costs they hadn't anticipated, including an unexpected and epic hike in gas prices. They very quickly began having trouble making ends meet on a day-to-day basis. Then, to make matters worse, one day not far into their travels they received a call from their oldest son informing them he was getting a divorce and asking if he could move in with them. And let's face it—three's a crowd in the ol' RV! In the end, they sold the RV (at a loss, of course) and resumed their former lives. It's a disappointing story and may very well have been avoided if they had taken a different approach in planning.

We want you to see your hopes and dreams happen just the

way you're envisioning them, and Step Two is the framework for the key components you'll need to turn your Prosperity Picture into a sustainable reality. Here we'll give you tools to take a realistic look at your current financial situation and also provide you with a preview of some basic financial building blocks that we'll cover in other parts of the book. Did you just get a little nervous reading that you'll be taking a *realistic* look at your financial situation? You're not alone. Many people get nervous here—but what we know is that the fear is almost always worse than the actuality of your financial situation.

Step One covered the first and most critical phase of helping you focus on what's most essential in your life and clarify your future vision. That's a very right-brain activity—meaning you drew heavily on the right hemisphere of your brain, which houses creative, visionary, and intuitive skills, essential in helping us determine where we would like to go. But the right hemisphere cannot act alone; it needs help getting to wherever that destination is. And that's where the left brain comes in. The left hemisphere houses our practical, tactical, and logical skills, perfectly suited to figure out how to turn our vision into reality. We need both hemispheres to work together in order to get the best outcome, and this chapter is your left brain's time to shine. So let's get it working.

Know What You Have and What You Owe

Often people who are successful in other parts of life neglect their financial wellness. Kathleen is a busy cardiologist who recently moved back to Chicago from Boston to work with a new medical group. At age forty-two, she decided the time had finally come to organize her finances, and with the assistance of her financial advisor took the first step by summarizing all of her investments. It turned out that in addition to the retirement plan she had with her current employer, Kathleen also had separate retirement accounts from three prior employers and bank accounts in three different cities. She had two mutual funds dating back to childhood that her parents had given her as gifts, with her mother still listed as the custodian.

As Kathleen was reviewing all of this on the initial statement prepared by her advisor, she remembered that she had some stock in her safe-deposit box that she hadn't included. When she retrieved the certificates, she realized the stock she had "forgotten about" was in IBM and was in fact worth more than $500,000! Now there's a good day, huh? This is a great example of the power of knowing what you have and what you owe.

Create a Written Inventory of Assets and Liabilities

Do you, right at this moment, have a clear idea of how much money you have and how much you owe? Is it pulled together in a financial inventory? Our compliments if you do; you're part of an elite group! Your next step is to go get it and take a look at it. Is it current? The details of our financial lives change frequently, so we recommend updating your inventory a minimum of twice a year in order to stay on top of things. (Don't do it more than once a month, though, because you'll drive yourself crazy if you do.) If you need to update it, take some time now to do that. If it's current and ready to go, you can skip this section.

If you're not sure of your specific financial details, you're not

alone—lots of people aren't. It can be tough to get started and difficult to keep up with. Our hope for you, however, is that you change
your thinking around this topic, because in order to move ahead
financially, you really have to know where you're starting.

You'll need about an hour to do this, and you'll also need access
to your financial information. If you handle your financial transac-
tions online, you'll need to be able to get to your computer as well.
If you're not able to do this now, grab your calendar or your Prosperity Notebook and write down a specific time, ideally within the
next week, when you'll do this.

Procrastinating? We get it. This relatively simple task is one
that many people spend their whole lives putting off, and we don't
want you to be one of them. This, along with the other topics in this
chapter, is a critical part of turning your vision into a reality.

There are two ways to go about this project: you can go digital
or you can go old school. If you're an online person, we suggest you
check out Mint.com. It's an online tool that you plug your key information into once and it then links to your bank, investment, and
other accounts and updates your information automatically. Computer software such as Quicken is another computer-based alternative that works well.

If you would rather keep it old school and do this with a pen
and paper, we've got everything you need right here. So let's get
started by completing your financial inventory. Go now to the
chapter appendix, pages 69–76, and fill this in as completely as
you can.

As you'll see, it begins with the positive side. What do you own?
Checking and savings account balances, credit union accounts,
other cash on hand. Then it provides blanks for any investment accounts you may own. Remember, this includes any retirement

accounts you might have at work, as well as accounts earmarked for kids' college. The last section is focused on physical assets: house, car, the resale value of personal property. We'll be honest: this can be tricky—it takes an inordinate amount of time to put a realistic resale value on a houseful of designer sofas, those lovely Moroccan tea glasses, and last season's gladiator sandals. And it can also be more than a little depressing to realize what these kinds of items are worth now compared with what you originally paid for them. The value of these smaller items is also not particularly important to your longer-term planning unless you intend to sell them at some point. To spare yourself the frustration, we suggest you focus primarily on the larger, more expensive items and do your best to assign a fair value to them. When you're finished, you'll have a complete list of where your money is now. These are your assets. Are you disappointed your asset number is not as high as you would like it to be? Don't be. Part of the value of doing this assessment is that it provides you with an honest look at the situation and allows you to move forward accordingly and make decisions on what you might want to do differently.

Next up is what you owe. This includes any loans you have— mortgage, car loan, student loans, and the like. For 39 percent of American families, this also includes credit card debt. Like weeds in the garden, high-interest credit card debt is something many people deal with on an ongoing basis. You probably know the scoop on debt. You've heard all the reasons why credit card debt is so vexing, you know credit card interest rates are not your friend, and you've seen the hypothetical illustrations showing you how the cost of financing even modestly priced goods with a credit card can be prohibitively expensive. Your fresh polenta with Maine lobster entrée that ostensibly cost $17.95 or your $249 forty-inch TV can actually cost considerably more by the time you're done financing it on a credit card with a 13 annual percent rate (APR). If you throw a lot of purchases "on the card" and pay only the minimum balance each month, you can easily fall into a dangerous financial trap.

A Look at Credit Card Debt

Maybe as you're reading this, you're thinking, "Well, I see the point, but really, is it that big of a deal? I know it's not ideal that I'm overpaying for my lobster or my TV, but is it worth all this fuss?" The answer, unequivocally, is *yes!*

Let's look at the hypothetical example of Jeannie, a thirtysomething woman with a live-in boyfriend who suddenly announces that "it's not her, it's him" and moves out. Jeannie is an unhappy camper. It's a financial stretch for her to stay in the apartment without his contribution, but she loves it and decides to stay. However, she hates that everything inside reminds her of him, so one weekend she decides to splurge on some throw pillows, towels, and other accessories to change things up. A thousand dollars later she's done, and her credit card bill that month totals $2,200—much more than normal. She could potentially scrimp and pay off the bill, but because she doesn't particularly feel like depriving herself in the midst of all this, she pays the attractive-looking minimum payment of $44 and feels fine.

Next month Jeannie splurges on a $2,000 watercolor she had been eyeing but that The Boyfriend never liked, and then she continues with some retail therapy and extra social activities to try to forget her emotional distress. When she gets her next bill, she's shocked to see a $7,000 balance! She had carried over the prior month's $2,156 balance and also spent *a lot* of money this past month. She can't even come close to paying off the bill this time, so once again pays the minimum and tries to forget about it. A few months down the road, the breakup starts to feel like less of a crisis, but she's left with a depressive ache. When friends suggest a pricey girls' trip to the Caribbean, she knows she can't really afford it but puts the $2,500 trip on her credit card anyway, then heads to the mall to go swimsuit shopping. At this point she's carrying a $10,000 balance on her credit card and has maxed it out. When she returns from her tropical getaway, cold, hard reality sets in—and she finally commits herself to stopping her overspending and to paying off her debt.

Jeannie's minimum payment is $200 a month (minimum payments are typically about 2 percent of the total amount owed) and her interest rate is 18 percent, which is also fairly standard. She does some quick math and guesstimates it might take about four years to get rid of the debt, as long as she pays the minimum and doesn't start spending again. But her guesstimate is woefully wrong! What she hadn't realized is that the card issuer will continue to apply more interest every single month until she pays back all the money. And here's the kicker: at the beginning of her payback period, the lion's share of her minimum payment is being applied to the interest she owes, not the principal (that is, the items she originally charged on her card). So, in the first year, 75 percent of her $200 ($150) is applied to the interest she already owes, and 25 percent ($50) goes to pay off the principal. Over the course of that first year, Jeannie will pay about $1,800 of interest and only $600 will go toward reducing her $10,000 balance. The principal will eventually shrink, but it will take a very long time. You can probably guess by now that there's no way Jeannie will pay off her debt in the four years she expects, but would you like to take a swing at how much her guesstimate is off? Making only the minimum monthly payment on her debt, Jeannie would need almost eight years to pay it off—about twice as long as she thought. Over that time she will have paid almost $9,000 in interest. We certainly hope those throw pillows were worth it!

Let's look at some better options. The good news is this: the enticing-looking minimum payment is a big, hairy trap. If she pays just a bit more than the minimum payment, things get better in a hurry. If, for example, she pays $300 a month (just an extra $25 a week beyond the minimum), she'll have the debt paid off in four years and will have shrunk her total interest to less than $4,000. If she pays $350 a month (an extra $37.50 per week beyond the minimum), she'll be done in just over three years and will have paid about $3,200 in interest. It's still a lot of time and money, but it's a heck of a lot better than eight years and nearly $9,000.

The bottom line: if you find yourself saddled with credit card debt, get rid of it ASAP! The more you can pay on a monthly basis to get rid of it, the better off you'll be. If you do have debt to pay off, don't waste your energy feeling stressed or ashamed. It happens— millions of people deal with this. Instead, let's focus on getting rid of it.

If you have credit card debt and carry it forward on a monthly basis, be clear on not only what you owe, but also on the interest you're being charged. Many credit cards charge anywhere between 12 and 19 percent interest, and even lowering your rate by a percentage point or two can make a huge difference. If you have credit card debt on multiple cards and aren't sure where to begin, you may want to consider consolidating your debt by either getting a loan with a lower interest rate to pay them off or by finding lower-interest-rate credit cards than you currently have and transferring your balances. If you choose to do this, be very careful. If you go with a loan, make sure the lender is reputable—there's a lot of fraudulent activity in this area. Check out the lender with the Better Business Bureau (see "Gain Traction Through Action" at the end of this chapter) and be especially cautious if the lender seems to be pressuring you into making a quick decision or not listening carefully to the details of your situation, both of which are red flags. If you transfer to a lower-rate credit card, make sure you read the fine print, understand the terms, and don't get stuck with a higher rate after the introductory period has ended. And also be aware that either approach may have a temporary negative impact on your credit scores.

Finishing Your Net Worth Calculation

Now back to our inventory. When you're finished, subtract your liabilities from your assets—what you owe from what you own—and you've just calculated your net worth. You may have a high number or you may have a negative number. If your number is low, you're not alone. About one in five households in the United States owes more in credit card debt, mortgages, car loans, and the like than they have in assets to back up the loans. If this is you, no judgments here. In fact, we applaud you for taking a good look at your situation—you now have a starting point to move ahead with your vision.

Now, if you're like the great majority of Americans, you would like to increase the net worth number you just calculated. One way you can accomplish that is by managing your spending. A lot of people refer to this as a budget, but we prefer to think of it as a "spending plan," which we find much more appealing than having a budget, which can seem like a bummer. We don't know many people who stick to budgets anyway. No one wants to eat celery sticks at a pizza party! A spending plan helps you look realistically at your monthly and annual expenses and provides you with a framework for spending as you move forward—which can be empowering. If you take it a step further and think about whether your current spending optimally reflects the things you really value in life, it can be even more empowering. We'll cover this idea in more depth in Chapter Six.

Now go to the chapter appendix one last time, on pages 71–76, to find the spending plan work sheet. As you fill it in, you'll notice there's a column that asks you to assign a priority level of A, B, or C to each item. Think of these labels as relating to how much you truly value the things or experiences in your life. A priorities relate to something you spend money on that is so important to you that you'd do whatever possible to make sure you could keep it in your life. B priorities are pretty darn important but not necessarily essential, while C's are nice to have but not necessary. For example, if your child's education is a high priority, mark saving for college as an A. You enjoy nice meals at restaurants very much, but you're willing to compromise if you have to—this one gets a B. And though you admit that it can sometimes be fun to have 344 cable TV channels available in your home, it wouldn't be a big deal to forgo them— here's a C.

Prioritizing expenses based upon your values is a much more impactful way to look at spending compared with the typical "fixed" versus "discretionary" budgeting process. Jessie is a good example of how this can be meaningful. She looked at her spending for the first time a couple of years ago. This was an exercise she'd always meant to do but never seemed to actually get around to doing. When she finally tracked what was flowing in and flowing out and where it was going, and honestly prioritized her spending, she decided to make some big life changes. Most people look at the expenses for their home as fixed, but Jessie realized she didn't really care much about her home now that her kids had moved out. Through this exercise she saw that her house and all the related expenses took up the majority of her cash flow each month. In order to pay for her lifestyle, she worked in a family business she hated. She hated her job so much that she found herself taking expensive vacations and running up credit card debt just to get away from the stress. So Jessie made a big decision. She decided to sell her house and pay off her mortgage, and then she bought a small condo (with a great view). This move saved her thousands of dollars a month. With the extra money, she paid off all of her credit card debt. With a much smaller nut to crack each month, Jessie took the risk of leaving her family business and starting her own consulting firm. She's happier than she's been in years.

You may choose to fill in the blanks in your Prosperity Notebook rather than in this book. Either way, you can use the spending plan work sheet as a guide. Just as with the financial inventory, you may have something like this already in place, in which case you'll just need to find it and make sure it's updated and accurate. Again, you may prefer to do this using online services or software, such as Mint.com or Quicken. Regardless, you'll need some time to do this. You'll also need access to a year's worth of credit card and bank statements so that you can complete it accurately. So if you don't have the time to do this now, grab your calendar and schedule a time to do so within the next week.

Take Your Financial Wellness Quiz

The next step is to do a status check on your financial wellness. This is a critical exercise to help you deepen your knowledge of where you are financially. It can be tempting to eyeball it and come to a quick conclusion that things are "okay," but do you really know? If you always wear elastic-waist pants (or in Lisa's case, her twelve-year-old relaxed-fit cargo skirt), how do you really know whether you've put on a few extra pounds or inches? Comfy as the cargo skirt may be, at some point you'll need to step on a scale or pull out the tape measure. Similarly, if you want to proactively design your financial life, you need to do a check on your basic financial wellness.

Do you have fond memories of being holed up in a friend's room or in the backseat on a road trip with a stash of junk food and a magazine quiz? Or is that just us? Regardless, we've got a quiz for you now. Below you'll find five easy questions about your satisfaction with some key areas of your financial wellness. The quiz should take you only a minute or two to complete. Please actually take it—once again, doing an honest self-assessment of these key factors is important if you want to move ahead in your financial life. You'll score yourself on a scale of 1 to 10 in each area, with 1 corresponding to "I have no clue" and 10 corresponding to "I am perfectly confident about this." Remember, nobody has to see your results if you don't want to share them, so be candid and honest with yourself. It's for your eyes only.

Financial Wellness Quiz

1) I am confident that my investment plan is allocated in a way that is appropriate for my goals.

Completely Disagree   Completely Agree

1   2   3   4   5   6   7   8   9   10   n/a

2) I am satisfied with the amount of money I'm currently saving/ investing.

Completely Disagree   Completely Agree

1   2   3   4   5   6   7   8   9   10   n/a

3) I communicate regularly and effectively with my spouse/partner about money (if applicable).

Completely Disagree   Completely Agree

1   2   3   4   5   6   7   8   9   10   n/a

4) I am confident that the insurance I have (health, life, home, auto, etc.) would adequately protect me if needed.

Completely Disagree   Completely Agree

1   2   3   4   5.   6   7   8   9   10   n/a

5) I have a will/estate plan that is complete and up-to-date.

Completely Disagree   **Completely Agree**

1   2   3   4   5   6   7   8   9   10   **n/a**

Evaluating Your Financial Wellness Quiz

Well, how did you do? Did you get perfect 10s across the board? Neither did we. Seriously, if you did give yourself a 10 in all five areas, congratulations—you're in an elite group of financial superstars!

More likely, you're in the same boat as the rest of us. You probably have good, solid scores in some areas, and in other areas, not so much. Or maybe you have work to do in all five areas. Regardless, our goal is to provide you with some ideas and guidance on how to get closer to a 10 in the areas in which you need the most help. How about those areas where you did have a 10? Or even an 8 or 9? No one is ever truly done improving in any area of life, but if you feel like a given area is working as well as it needs to, maybe it makes more sense to focus on areas of greater need. If that's the case, feel free to skip those sections. It's up to you.

Before we delve into our first area, let's cover what you can expect in general. This book is meant to be a resource for you. We've provided Web sites, online calculators, and some tools right here in the book that you can use to work through these issues. You could read your way through volumes and volumes about any one of these five areas and still not scratch the surface—they're that broad. Therefore, our intention is to put the most important elements for you personally on your radar screen, and then give you some basic tools and resources you can access later to further address your needs. This process will be easier if you create an "Action Plan" for yourself now to use as a central place to note what specific steps make sense for you to investigate. Just grab your Prosperity Notebook, turn to a fresh sheet, and write "Action Plan" at the top. Keep it handy so you can jot down action items as they occur to you. We think you'll find that, with a small amount of effort in each of these areas, you can expect to see big results.

Area One: Allocate Your Investment Plan to Help You Meet Your Goals

In order to help meet your long-term goals, it's important to own the "right mix" of different categories of investments, such as stocks in differently sized companies, bonds (loans to companies, governments, or municipalities), commodities (investments in physical substances, like gold or oil), and cash. The right mix is different for everybody, and that's because we all need to make sure we match our investments with our individual risk comfort level and our long-term needs. Sometimes there is a mismatch. For example, if an investor is too aggressive in her investment choices, her portfolio value may fluctuate greatly and cause worry, indigestion, and sleepless nights. This angst might cause her to make emotional decisions to relieve this worry but that could hurt her long-term financial progress. On the flip side, investing too conservatively may impede her chances of reaching long-term goals.

Asset allocation, sometimes known as diversification, refers to putting money into broad categories of investments. There is often confusion around this—diversification does not refer to spreading your money out among different investment companies, financial advisors, or banks. It doesn't even necessarily refer to spreading it out over different stocks, bonds, or mutual funds. It refers to spreading it across broad investment categories, such as investments in small, medium, and large U.S. companies, investments in foreign companies, bonds, commodities, and commercial real estate. The reality is, there is no way to predict exactly which categories will perform well in any given year. But there is a way to use asset allocation techniques that, though no guarantee of future success, have been effective in increasing the chances of making money and decreasing the chances of losing money in the past. We'll delve into this subject in Chapter Three.

Area Two: Save and Invest the Right Amount for Yourself

The first question to ask yourself is whether you're completely clear on how much you're saving. Our friend Patricia is brilliant. She has a successful career as a management consultant, a beautiful family of four, and a magnificent house in Chicago straight out of a magazine. When a financial planner asked her what her salary was, she smiled brightly, said, "I don't know," and took a sip of coffee. She had an idea of the general range, but she really didn't know the specific number. Nor was she exactly sure of how much she and her husband had in their investment accounts or how much she was contributing to her retirement accounts.

Depending on your personality type, this may seem silly to you, but it's not unusual. We are all busy people who juggle multiple demands and this information is not always top of mind. So question number one is simply this: when you add up all of the savings and investing accounts that you contribute to regularly, what are you on track to accrue on a monthly and yearly basis? Remember, this includes your savings in any retirement plans at work such as a 401(k) or 403(b) plan, any matching you receive from your employer, any other retirement awards like stock or deferred compensation, as well as any savings you accumulate outside of retirement accounts. If you manage money with a significant other, this number will obviously include their savings and contributions as well.

And . . . Are You Sure That's the Right Number for You?

Once you know what you are actually saving, the second question is whether you're confident it's the right amount to help you reach your goals. A common question is, "How much should I be saving on a monthly or annual basis?" It's tempting to want to stick with a consistent percentage, such as 10 or 20 percent of your gross income (numbers often cited as savings rates to shoot for). But that can be a trap. Aiming for 10 to 20 percent might be a good range for you, or it might be wildly high or low depending completely on your personal situation and what your goals are for the future. Maybe you've got big plans for retirement. Or maybe you plan on scaling down and living very simply. Do you have kids or grandkids whom you would like to help with college? Do you have a goal of buying a vacation home or a boat? Of starting a charitable foundation? Lisa's husband Tony has a tin piggy bank that says, "I'm saving up to be a rock star." (Which, in his case, is more or less true!)

Is there a vocation or hobby that you need to build up money to pursue?

All of these questions obviously factor into your monthly savings plans. What do you want from your future and how much will it cost? Once you know this, you can focus on what you need to work toward on a monthly basis to stay on track. We will be looking at this question in detail in Chapter Four.

Area Three: Communicate Regularly and Effectively with Your Spouse or Partner About Money

The first year they were married, Lisa and her husband got into a big argument over the cost of . . . wait for it . . . a Christmas tree! We know countless shoppers who immediately remove the tags from new items so their partner won't know they spent money on something new. Our friend Elaine micromanages her husband's financial activity to such an extent that she once called him at work to ask if he had sustained a $2.50 ATM charge. All of these are pretty small potatoes. What about big disconnects about how much should be saved or spent, how much risk to take with investments, how much to spend on a vacation or a new car? Money can hold a powerful charge in relationships—and that charge can be used in a positive or a negative way. Most of us think first about the negative—experts say conflicts about money lead more couples to divorce than any other reason. Yet, ironically, openly communicating about money can also be a wonderful way for couples to build a strong foundation for reaching joint goals, as we've already explored. Because we believe in the power of being positive, we'll offer more ways you can build the strongest financial foundation possible. Not convinced household finance is romantic? Which sounds better: walking the path of your financial life hand in hand with your partner, or otherwise fighting about it, leaving a partner lost if you die unexpectedly, or finding yourself overwhelmed if you face a sudden divorce? In Chapter Four, we'll share thoughts and ideas on how to approach this topic in a way that will help you live the best life you can with your significant other.

Not Sure Your Partner Is Willing to Do This with You?

If you just read this and thought, "Well, that would be great, but I just don't see it happening with the two of us," you're not alone. We meet plenty of people who are in this situation with their significant other. Sometimes one partner doesn't think this kind of conversation is important and that things are fine as they are. Some are just not interested—they find it boring. Or they never have the time. If you find yourself in this situation for any reason at all, make sure to start with the Couples Prosperity Picture and shared vision we covered in Chapter One before you move into the nuts-and-bolts issues (the "basics"), which we cover in Chapter Four. Even though the basics are more fundamental, the shared vision is more exciting and accessible, and may be useful in getting your partner enthused and on board. It's intoxicating to envision the exciting life the two of you could share down the road! You can circle back to the basics later.

Area Four: Have the Right Insurance to Protect Yourself and Your Family

Have you seen the early-nineties film *Fried Green Tomatoes*? There's a scene in which one of the main characters, Evelyn, an "older" woman, is waiting for a parking spot, only to have two young girls in another car nose in front of her and steal it. Evelyn says, "Excuse me, I was waiting for that space!" and one of the girls says, "Face it, lady, we're younger and faster!" Evelyn looks at them for a moment, presses her foot onto the accelerator, and deliberately bashes into the back of their car. She proceeds to do it again several times, wrecking the entire vehicle. Then she looks at them and says, "Face it, girls, I'm older and I have more insurance." Indeed, insurance can be an empowering thing.

In all seriousness, insurance serves a critical purpose: it puts a safety net under your plan. You can do the best financial planning in the world, but if a family member needs extended long-term care that you need to pay for out of pocket, if someone in your family has an accident or health issue you need to cover, or if someone on whose income stream you are depending passes away unexpectedly, it can blow your plan out of the water. Likewise, if your family is relying on your income and, heaven forbid, you were to become disabled or pass away without the proper insurance, *they* could be left in real trouble.

For most people, this is neither a fun nor sexy topic, but even that can change. Lisa was at a brunch with a group of friends she's known for nearly twenty years—all women who have more or less "grown up" together. When they were in their twenties, the brunch conversation was often about exactly what you might think . . . last night's men, tonight's dinner destination, and maybe what movie to see. Now, well past their twenties, they may still indulge in a bit of that chat (after all, we're not dead yet!), but sprinkled in is a healthy dose of chatter about umbrella insurance and health care plans— enough that we marvel we've come to this point: where the party talk is about insurance! No matter how dry the subject is, though, insurance is something everyone has to face. And we're confident you'll find that the more thoroughly you address your insurance needs, the easier you'll sleep at night and the more financially re-silient you'll become. In Chapter Six, we'll look at this in more de-tail.

Area Five: Have a Will or Estate Plan
That Is Complete and Up-to-Date

We know of a man, Larry, who owned farmland, barns, and per-sonal property valued in excess of a million dollars. He had several children and in his will stipulated simply that he would like his as-sets to be divided evenly among them. He left it to them to figure out exactly how that would happen and appointed the eldest son to be in charge. When he passed away, his heirs immediately began arguing about how to divide the property . . . and they're still argu-ing nearly ten years later! All of the property and assets have been sitting in limbo this entire time. Meanwhile, one of Larry's sons passed away himself. The deceased son's immediate family, who could have used some extra money to pay for his grandchildren's education, cannot access their inheritance. The oldest son, who's "in charge," has a drinking problem and has let crucial administrative duties, such as paying property tax, lapse, causing some of the as-sets to be lost to government seizure. It's a hot mess, and certainly couldn't be what this man would have wanted for his family. Let's make sure you and your heirs avoid this kind of difficulty.

This is no one's favorite subject—understandably so. Who likes to think about their own mortality? As a result, this area of planning gets avoided like no other—49 percent of Americans don't have an estate plan. If you don't have one, we understand. But we also need you to know that it's not okay. It's important to take the responsibility for making your wishes clear. Who will make decisions for you if you can't do it yourself? If you have kids, who will care for them? What would you like to see happen to your assets and belongings? What charities would you like to support? Think of writing these things down as a love letter to the people you care about most. What's more, if you don't send that love letter, whether you intend to or not, you'll put those people in a terribly difficult situation. We'll cover some estate planning basics in Chapter Six.

Finally, a brief word on that term "estate." It's a bit intimidating, isn't it? It may call to mind a ten-bedroom mansion on the coast with tennis courts and a kennel. But don't let that fool you— it's just a legal term used to describe your property. It doesn't matter whether your property consists of a nice shoe collection and some family photos, a quiet house in the suburbs, or a fancy place like the one mentioned above. You still need to clarify what you would like to happen to it.

Pulling the Building Blocks Together

The concepts we've covered in this chapter are the financial building blocks for your future: having an accurate idea of what you own and what you owe, working toward saving and investing the right amount for your needs, having the right insurance coverage, having an estate plan in place, communicating about money as effectively as possible with your significant other (if that's relevant for you), and having the right asset allocation in place for any investments you currently own. Remember, the goal of this chapter is to put the most relevant issues for you onto your radar screen. As we move through the book, we'll provide you with more information about each of the five key areas on the quiz. Again, you could read your way through volumes and volumes about any one of these five areas and still not scratch the surface, because they're so broad. So the goal here is to help you develop a good strong "Action Plan" for yourself with a list of next steps that are most important for you to pursue by the time you finish this book. These are subjects many people spend their whole lives ignoring. Don't let yourself fall into that trap. With just a small amount of effort in each of these areas, you can see big results—and that journey, of course, begins with the very first step.

Gain Traction Through Action

• Create an inventory of your assets and liabilities. List what you own and owe, then subtract what you owe from what you own. Track these numbers at least two times per year, but not more than once a month.

• Complete (or review) your spending plan. This information will be super helpful as you are creating your plan.

• Got debt? Be deliberate about reducing interest charges and increasing your payments. Use an online credit card repayment calculator to help. If you are considering using a credit counseling service, make sure to check them out with the Better Business Bureau (www.bbb.org).

• Take the Financial Wellness Quiz. Think about the areas of biggest opportunity for you.

• Create an Action Plan in your Prosperity Notebook. This will serve as an ongoing list for you to note items you want to handle, tackle, and learn more about.

Chapter Two Appendix

Assets and Liabilities Inventory

CASH   VALUE

- Cash on hand $_____

- Checking account balance $_____

- Savings account balance $_____

- Certificates of deposit $_____

- Money market account balance $_____

- Credit union account balance $_____

- Money owed to you $_____

- Cash value of life insurance $_____

- Other $_____

INVESTMENTS/RETIREMENT ACCOUNTS

- Stocks/bonds $_____

- Mutual fund shares $_____

- Retirement plan $_____

- IRA account $_____

- Profit sharing plan $_____

- Treasury bills $_____

- Annuity $_____
- Investment real estate equity $_____
- 529 plan $_____
- Other $_____

PERSONAL

- Home fair market value $_____
- Cars $_____
- Furniture $_____
- Other personal property $_____
- Jewelry/art/collectibles $_____
- Other $_____

TOTAL ASSETS $_____

LIABILITIES   AMOUNT

- Mortgage $_____
- Car loan(s) $_____
- Installment loan(s) $_____
- Credit card debt $_____
- Student loan(s) $_____
- Personal loan(s) $_____

- Other $_____

TOTAL LIABILITIES $_____

DETERMINE YOUR NET WORTH

- Total assets $_____

- **Minus total liabilities** $_____

NET WORTH $_____

SPENDING PLAN

INCOME	MONTHLY	ANNUALLY
Salary	_____	_____
Salary	_____	_____
Bonus	_____	_____
TOTAL INCOME	$_____	$_____
Federal Taxes	_____	_____
State Taxes	_____	_____
Social Security & Medicare Taxes	_____	_____
TOTAL TAXES	$_____	$_____
NET INCOME	$_____	$_____

(total income less total taxes)

CONTRIBUTIONS TO SAVINGS/INVESTMENT ACCOUNTS	MONTHLY	ANNUALLY
401(k)/403(b) plan	_____	_____
IRA	_____	_____
College savings	_____	_____
Other savings/investing	_____	_____
TOTAL SAVINGS	$_____	$_____

EXPENSES (HOUSING)	MONTHLY	ANNUALLY	PRIORITY (A, B, C)
Mortgage/rent	_____	_____	_____
Real estate taxes	_____	_____	_____
Condo Fees	_____	_____	_____
Gas/water/electric	_____	_____	_____
Home insurance	_____	_____	_____
Improvements	_____	_____	_____
Maintenance	_____	_____	_____
Security	_____	_____	_____
Telephone	_____	_____	_____
Cable/Internet	_____	_____	_____
Cleaning service	_____	_____	_____
Other	_____	_____	_____
TOTAL HOUSING EXPENSES	$_____	$_____	

EXPENSES (FOOD)	MONTHLY	ANNUALLY	PRIORITY (A, B, C)
Dining out	_____	_____	_____
Groceries	_____	_____	_____
Liquor	_____	_____	_____
Other	_____	_____	_____
TOTAL FOOD EXPENSES	$_____	$_____	

EXPENSES (HEALTH)	MONTHLY	ANNUALLY	PRIORITY (A, B, C)
Life insurance	_____	_____	_____
Disability insurance	_____	_____	_____
Long term care insurance	_____	_____	_____
Medical insurance	_____	_____	_____
Doctor/dentist	_____	_____	_____
Medicine	_____	_____	_____
Vision care	_____	_____	_____
Other	_____	_____	_____
TOTAL HEALTH EXPENSES	$_____	$_____	

EXPENSES (TRANSPORTATION)	MONTHLY	ANNUALLY	PRIORITY (A, B, C)
Lease/auto loan payments	_____	_____	_____
Maintenance	_____	_____	_____
License/fees	_____	_____	_____

	MONTHLY	ANNUALLY	PRIORITY (A, B, C)
Insurance	_____	_____	_____
Parking	_____	_____	_____
Train/bus/taxi	_____	_____	_____
Other	_____	_____	_____
TOTAL TRANSPOR-TATION EXPENSES	$_____	$_____	

EXPENSES (EDUCATION)	MONTHLY	ANNUALLY	PRIORITY (A, B, C)
Tuition	_____	_____	_____
Books/materials	_____	_____	_____
Dues/fees	_____	_____	_____
School loan repayments	_____	_____	_____
Other	_____	_____	_____
TOTAL EDUCATION EXPENSES	$_____	$_____	

EXPENSES (CHILDREN)	MONTHLY	ANNUALLY	PRIORITY (A, B, C)
Child care	_____	_____	_____
Lessons/activities	_____	_____	_____
Camp	_____	_____	_____
Clothing	_____	_____	_____
Other	_____	_____	_____
TOTAL CHILDREN EXPENSES	$_____	$_____	

EXPENSES (PERSONAL)	MONTHLY	ANNUALLY	PRIORITY (A, B, C)
Grooming (salon, barber, nails, etc.)	_____	_____	_____
Toiletries/cosmetics	_____	_____	_____
Clothing	_____	_____	_____
Cleaning/laundry	_____	_____	_____
Gifts/holidays	_____	_____	_____
Charitable contributions	_____	_____	_____
Counseling/therapy	_____	_____	_____
Pet care	_____	_____	_____
Financial advisor	_____	_____	_____
Accountant	_____	_____	_____
Safe-deposit box	_____	_____	_____
Credit card/personal debt repayment	_____	_____	_____
Other	_____	_____	_____
TOTAL PERSONAL EXPENSES	$_____	$_____	

EXPENSES (ENTERTAINMENT)	MONTHLY	ANNUALLY	PRIORITY (A, B, C)
Club memberships	_____	_____	_____
Hobbies	_____	_____	_____
Subscriptions	_____	_____	_____
Recreation/sports	_____	_____	_____
Theater	_____	_____	_____

	MONTHLY	ANNUALLY	PRIORITY (A, B, C)
Vacation	_____	_____	_____
Other	_____	_____	_____
TOTAL ENTERTAINMENT EXPENSES	$_____	$_____	
TOTAL EXPENSES	$_____	$_____	
NET INCOME	$_____	$_____	
MINUS TOTAL SAVINGS	$_____	$_____	
MINUS TOTAL LIVING EXPENSES	$_____	$_____	
UNALLOCATED AMOUNT	$_____	$_____	

Chapter Three

Step Three:
Design a Winning Plan

Do you remember Tamara from the introduction? The fashion retailer who overcame a serious childhood medical condition and
went on to build a rewarding life for herself? As you may recall,
Tamara points to visualization as a major contributor to her success,
and even though visualization is hugely powerful, she knew it
wasn't enough in and of itself to turn her vision into a reality. After
she set her sights on owning the retail clothing shop that she would
eventually name Clever Alice, Tamara created a plan. She began
training and educating herself by working at existing shops she ad-
mired in Chicago. She spent her free time researching and learning
how to develop a business plan. She crunched numbers to determine how much she could afford in rent, how many salespeople she
could afford to hire, how much inventory she could carry, and what
sales volume she would need to do to sustain the shop. She explored
the market to understand who her competition was and what lines
she could bring in to make an impact in Chicago. And then she
combined it all into a comprehensive plan and told herself she would
go out and actually create "this or something better"—build either
the business detailed in the plan or a more successful version of it.

How do you move your vision of your future life into a reality? In Chapter One, you used visual images to create your financial and life vision. You stimulated the intuitive, visual part of your brain by choosing the images you're attracted to and putting them together to create your personal Prosperity Picture. In Chapter Two, you did your "reality check" on some critical areas of financial planning. Now we're going to create a tangible forward-looking plan together.

And here's some more good news: this plan is not going to be a yawn-inducing seventy-two-page document, a ten-part spreadsheet, or an "easy" software system that takes all weekend to install on your computer. Instead, it begins with building on your Prosperity Picture. You'll need that, along with your Prosperity Notebook, to move ahead with this chapter, so please get them now.

Moving from Picture to Reality

Even though the subconscious mind is incredibly powerful, we need to get our conscious mind in on the action too. So let's look at some tangible ways to move the ideas on your Prosperity Picture into reality. You should have a variety of images on your picture board representing many parts of life. Pick one, preferably from your "Sooner/More Money" section, to get started. Grab your pen and Prosperity Notebook, write "Goals List" at the top of a fresh page, and answer the following "Picture Planning" questions:

- What specific goal does this picture suggest to you?
- What's your estimate of the financial resources you'll need to make it happen?

- What's the time frame in which you would ideally like to see your goal happen?
- What other people are involved?
- What other information do you need?
- What is the first step you need to take (or the next step)?

Let's use the waterfall image as an example. What specific goal does it represent? It might mean a getaway trip to Hawaii. Approximate cost? Two people could probably reasonably fly there, stay at a nice hotel, and enjoy some excursions (including the very important waterfall!) for $5,000 to $7,000 (or cheaper if you looked for deals). Time frame? Let's assume you don't have an extra $5,000 to $7,000 lying around. If that's the case, you may not be sure of the timing, but ideally it would be sometime in the next two years. What other people are involved? In this example, it would just be you and your partner. What other information do you need? Maybe some expert travel tips? Perhaps you have a friend who might have recommendations or tips for saving money on the trip or maybe you do research online. And the first step? How about setting up a "Hawaii fund" today? It can be as simple as a savings or investment account earmarked just for this purpose. You are now officially on your way! You still don't have your $5,000 to $7,000, and you're not in Kona yet, but it seems much more like a real possibility already now that you've specified what you need to plan for. In short, you've created momentum.

Once you begin thinking in this fashion, you'll probably find it somewhat addictive, in a good way. So keep going. Pick a new image every couple of days, once a week, once a month—whatever makes sense to you—and walk through these questions. Record the answers in your Prosperity Notebook. Remember, each minute you spend doing this is a minute that potentially pushes those images on your Prosperity Picture closer to becoming a reality.

Prioritizing Your Goals

Once you begin focusing on your Prosperity Picture and working through your Goals List regularly, you will probably find that a few of the images or ideas keep popping up as being especially appealing. Those are the ones to focus on first. It can be overwhelming—impossible even—to think about funding everything on your Picture at once, so begin with one to three of them for the funding process.

You may be thinking, "I have so many things I'm excited about—how do I choose what to focus on first?" We suggest you start with a goal you would like to see happen sooner and one that requires some money and planning, but not necessarily a huge amount of money. This will help build your planning muscles. Once you walk through this process, you'll then be able to more easily approach the longer-term, more complex, and more costly goals (such as planning for retirement).

It is also a good idea to tap into your inner wisdom when it comes to setting priorities. Focus on what's truly important to you (and to your partner if you are planning with someone else). Spend some time soaking in the images on your Prosperity Picture from a quiet, calm place and begin to prioritize your goals. When Ellen asks her teenagers what they want and they say, "I don't know," she usually responds, "If you did know, what would it be?" So if you're not sure which goal you want to start with, try asking yourself, "If I did know, what would it be?"

Mary's Story

It's amazing what you can achieve when you take an intentional approach to planning and working toward your goals. Our friend Mary is a thirty-five-year-old social worker and college instructor living in Chicago. Many years ago she created her own version of a Goals List, which included things she wanted to accomplish in her lifetime. She made an agreement with herself to accomplish one thing on the list each year. Among the things on Mary's list:

• Buy the home she'd always wanted in downtown Chicago: two bedrooms, lots of space, and an aesthetically pleasing interior.
• Adopt a dog—she's a huge dog lover!
• Help her nephew pay for college.

Using these lifetime goals as a basis, Mary created her Prosperity Picture. She placed the paintbrush and swatch image, which represents her condo, in the middle of her "Sooner/More Money" box. The dog and cat image is in her "Sooner/Less Money" box. (Dog people: we know you may not be thrilled that there's a cat sitting right next to the dog on the picture. And vice versa for you cat folks. If it makes you feel better, go ahead and snip out whichever animal you don't like—people do it in workshops all the time!) Mary is completely smitten with her four-year-old nephew Arthur and wants to contribute to his college fund, so she placed the image of the big extended family in the "Later/More Money" box to represent that. She has many more images on her board, but these three goals are particularly important to her. Let's take a look at how she went after them.

Based on some initial real estate scouting, Mary determined

that she could probably find the condo she had in mind for between $250,000 and $300,000. She looked into mortgage options and learned that she could qualify for a loan with a 20 percent down payment. She had already saved $20,000, so she set a goal to save an additional $40,000. She estimated that, based on rates at the time, her monthly house payment, including mortgage, property tax, and condo association fees, would likely be between $1,500 and $2,000—just slightly more than she was paying for rent. So the trick for her was getting together the down payment, and she really wanted to have the place within three years. Her goal, then, was to save $40,000 within three years.

Now for the dog. Mary planned to adopt her dog from a shelter—a minimal cost of about $200, but she estimated it would require about $1,200 a year to care for her dog (emergencies aside). She knew she could cover the $100 a month from her regular cash flow. Time frame? ASAP.

Her nephew's college fund is harder to plan for. She has no idea what the cost of tuition will be fourteen years from now; however, she's planning to help—not pay the entire tab—so she doesn't need to have all the answers. She doesn't currently have a lot of extra income to gift, so she decides to put aside money as she can and give it to Arthur in increments of $50 to $100 for birthdays and holidays. She believes her income will increase later in her career, which will allow her to give him larger gifts and perhaps establish an investment account for him. Time frame? If all goes according to plan for Arthur, she has fourteen years for this one!

Mary established two short-term goals and one long-term goal. What did she do next? The dog goal was easy—she had the $200 to adopt her dog and knew she could cover the $100 per month in care costs out of her regular monthly cash flow. So she went straight to the shelter to meet some dogs in need of a home. Within a few months, Mary was the proud owner of Bella, who is now a happy, healthy, and, according to Mary, "very spoiled" canine.

The condo was obviously much more expensive and also trickier. She sat down with a calculator and determined she needed to save a bit more than $1,100 a month to accrue her $40,000 down payment within three years. Mary's job as a social worker falls into the category of a noble calling that unfortunately isn't as lucrative as it should be, and accruing an extra $1,100 a month was out of reach. She realized the only way to make it happen would be to earn more income, and the only way to do that would be to get a second job. Mary had earned an advanced degree as part of her social work training and was qualified to teach related college-level courses, so she made a decision to teach an undergraduate psychology class in addition to maintaining her full-time job. This impressive decision meant a significant increase in workload and definitely took a bite out of her free time, but she kept her eye on the prize and did it. Mary's vision, planning, and can-do attitude paid off. Though she wasn't quite able to reach the goal of an extra $1,100 per month, she was able to save $850 per month. So she didn't meet her three-year goal, but within four years she moved into her beautiful new two-bedroom condo in one of Chicago's most vibrant neighborhoods.

Mary's goal to contribute to her nephew Arthur's college fund currently consists of an extra $50 or $100 in months when Mary is able to put it aside. As he gets older, and as Mary's earnings increase, she anticipates this amount increasing and perhaps becoming a more formal arrangement.

Her story is a great example of how to turn Prosperity Picture goals into reality. But all of her calculations were based simply on saving cash. The next step is to look at ways to invest the money and potentially generate extra return.

The Magic of Compound Interest

Take a look at the following illustration—the glorious compound interest chart. This is the perfect place to begin our discussion of investing. Maybe you've seen one before. Whether you have or haven't, it's a beautiful thing to behold. It can be truly amazing to look at the potential for money to grow over time, even at relatively modest rates of return.

COMPOUND INTEREST
HYPOTHETICAL GROWTH CHART

$200 MONTHLY INVESTMENT

	0% annual return	2% annual return	4% annual return	6% annual return
Year 1	$2,400	$2,426	$2,452	$2,477
Year 5	$12,000	$12,625	$13,279	$13,965
Year 10	$24,000	$26,563	$29,435	$32,653
Year 15	$36,000	$41,952	$49,092	$57,662
Year 20	$48,000	$58,944	$73,007	$91,129
Year 25	$60,000	$77,703	$102,103	$135,916

$2,000 MONTHLY INVESTMENT

	0% annual return	2% annual return	4% annual return	6% annual return
Year 1	$24,000	$24,259	$24,517	$24,773
Year 5	$120,000	$126,246	$132,791	$139,648
Year 10	$240,000	$265,632	$294,352	$326,529
Year 15	$360,000	$419,525	$490,916	$576,617
Year 20	$480,000	$589,435	$730,066	$911,292
Year 25	$600,000	$777,030	$1,021,028	$1,359,162

$10,000 MONTHLY INVESTMENT

	0% annual return	2% annual return	4% annual return	6% annual return
Year 1	$120,000	$121,296	$122,584	$123,865
Year 5	$600,000	$631,230	$663,957	$698,240
Year 10	$1,200,000	$1,328,158	$1,471,762	$1,632,643
Year 15	$1,800,000	$2,097,623	$2,454,580	$2,883,085
Year 20	$2,400,000	$2,947,175	$3,650,329	$4,556,458
Year 25	$3,000,000	$3,885,149	$5,105,140	$6,795,808

Source: FINRA Savings Calculator

Important information about this calculation: These returns are not adjusted for inflation. This calculation evaluates basic savings scenarios, not complex ones where deposits start and stop at varying intervals. Deposits are made at the beginning of the month or year and shown through month end or year end. Interval periods are of equal length, so results do not apply to scenarios with actual calendar-based periods. Rates of return and inflation remain the same each year. This tool does not account for taxes. If it did, results would be much lower. Some products may include fees that this tool does not consider. All results are hypothetical so your results will be higher or lower than those shown.

Compound interest is very simple. It's a way to build wealth over time by regularly putting aside a specific amount of money and leaving it to potentially grow. Take a minute to really look at the possible numbers. It doesn't take long to realize that time is on your side when it comes to saving and investing. Look at what can happen if you invest $200 a month every month for twenty-five years. Even if you put it into an account that provides no earnings at all, your $200 will build to $60,000 at the end of the twenty-five years. But it gets really exciting when you add the "interest" part into the equation. If you invest your $200 a month into an account that returns an average of 6 percent a year, you can potentially turn it into almost $136,000 at the end of those twenty-five years. All you have to do is continue to make your $200 monthly investment, leave any earnings right in the account, and let it do its thing. As long as your average annual return stays at 6 percent per year, you'll get to your $136,000. Not bad!

If you're in your twenties or younger, compound interest really rocks—time is on your side. Ellen explained this to her son Benjy as they were talking about his summer jobs. Benjy estimated that between his two jobs he might earn close to $4,000. She shared with him that if he were to take this money and put it into a Roth IRA so that he wouldn't have to pay taxes on this money, and continue to do this each year until he was out of college, he would have saved a total of $16,000. If he invested this money and was able to earn 6 percent on it, by the time he was sixty-five he would have over $200,000. If he continued to save $4,000 per year, by age sixty-five he would have accumulated more than $1 million! Now, this assumes he won't spend any of his summer job earnings while he's in college, which is not realistic, but this big number certainly motivated Benjy to put away as much as possible.

Whether you're twenty-five or ninety-five, you've got the potential to make relatively small amounts of money grow into something great. (One note: the numbers on the chart are not adjusted for inflation, so be aware that even though the numbers on the chart are significant, the money won't go as far twenty-five years from now as it will today.)

If you have more to work with, it gets even better. Investing $2,000 a month at a 6 percent potential rate of return annually will turn into $1.3 million in twenty-five years. If you are lucky enough to have $10,000 a month to invest over twenty-five years, you can potentially grow it to nearly $7 million at a 6 percent average annual return. Think of the possibilities!

Small decisions about your money on a daily basis can significantly influence your financial situation over time. Saving or investing $200 a month comes down to only $6 or $7 a day. Think about the things that might compel you to spend $6 or $7 (or more) over the course of a day. What's your pleasure? A samosa from the food truck? A mojito? Your latest guilty-pleasure celeb mag? What if you didn't indulge in those things every time you felt the urge? What if you brought your lunch, drank water, or turned to the Internet for celebrity gossip? Now let's be clear: we're not telling you to give up *all* of the things that bring you pleasure. We're not into deprivation, and we like samosas, mojitos, and a nice glossy magazine as much as the next girl. Not to mention the fact that we (well, Lisa) aren't the best at self-discipline sometimes. But the point is, it's an opportunity for each of us to make a different decision each day if we want to. At a 6 percent rate of return, $7 a day could potentially get you more than $32,000 in ten years; $67 a day could get you more than $326,000 in those ten years; and if you're fortunate enough to be able to put aside $333 a day, you could accrue $1.6 million in that decade. Take a moment and think about how this concept relates to you. Then take a look at the compound interest chart again and think about it some more!

Investment Options for Short-term Financial Goals

Now let's look at goals you want to accomplish in less than five years. It makes sense to work toward those by using lower-risk investments, meaning investments that have some potential for growth but that may also have less risk of losing money in the short run—after all, you have plans for this money, so you want it to be there for you when you need it. Many people simply use bank savings accounts (which may offer a small return on the money held within the account) or their current income sources for short-term goals. But there are some other options worthy of consideration.

Money Market or Savings Accounts

Money market or savings accounts typically offer a low rate of return on your money for a very low amount of risk. Interest rates fluctuate on these accounts, so it's worth it to shop around to check current rates. A quick online search using Bankrate.com or a similar Web site can give you an overview of rates. Also remember that, though historically rare, it is possible to lose money invested in some types of money market accounts.

Certificates of Deposit (CDs)

A CD is a time deposit. When you invest in a CD, you make a commitment to keep your money invested, typically between six months and five years, and it will pay you interest until the term ends. A CD is less flexible than a savings or money market account. You can't add to or withdraw from it during the term, and if you cash in your CD before it matures, you'll probably need to pay a penalty (often three months of interest). To make up for the inconvenience of tying up your money, CDs typically pay higher interest than savings or money market accounts (but not always), with the highest rates for the longest terms.

Short-term Bond Funds

A bond is a loan that an investor makes to a government, municipality, corporation, or other similar institution. In exchange for the use of your money, the institution agrees to repay the loan with interest at a set maturity date. Bonds are fixed-income securities because many pay you interest based on a predetermined rate—also called a coupon rate—which is set when the bond is issued. A bond *fund* is a "basket" of multiple bonds, chosen by a professional money management team, that can hold anywhere from thirty or forty individual bonds all the way up to hundreds of them.

Short-term bond mutual funds may be a good fit for your

"sooner" category goals because they can potentially offer a better return than savings accounts, money market funds, or CDs. Keep in mind, though, that even though bonds have historically been less volatile than other types of investments, you still run a risk that your investment may end up being worth less than you put into the account. As with all investments, make sure you fully understand what you're buying before you invest.

So which one of these short-term options is best for you? If you would like to see your money potentially grow at a higher (though still relatively low) rate, and you're willing to take a small amount of risk, short-term bond funds may be best. If you would prefer to keep the risk as minimal as possible, then a savings account, money market fund, or CD would be better for you. A CD usually provides slightly better interest rates than a money market, which is obviously preferable, but the trade-off is that you'll have to commit to keeping your money tied up for the term of the CD. So take a look at your time frame and also at any other financial obligations that may require you to access your money. If you're fairly certain you can leave your money invested in the CD for the entire term, that's probably the best option for you. Bottom line: depending on how much money you're looking to build up and how much risk you're willing to take, any of these options can potentially turn the "Sooner" items on your Prosperity Picture into reality.

Investment Options for Long-term Financial Goals

Now let's look at the right half of your Prosperity Picture: the longer-term goals. These are life objectives that you see happening later on, five or more years from now. For most people, pursuing longer-term financial goals means investing in the stock market (or "equities") in some form or fashion. When you think of investing in the stock market, what's your first reaction? If your answer is "That seems risky," "Just thinking about it makes me nervous," or "There's not a snowball's chance in hell," you're not alone. Plenty of people feel anxious at the mere mention of investing in the stock market.

But there is another side to the story. If you're like most people, you've worked hard for your money, and in turn you would like your money to work hard for you. Right? Well, here's the thing: historically, one of the best ways for investors to grow their money has been to invest in the stock market.

Let's Talk Stocks and Mutual Funds . . . Just for a Minute

A stock is an ownership share of a company. Are you a fan of Louis Vuitton handbags? If you are, you can own a part of the company by purchasing shares of LVMH Moët Hennessy Louis Vuitton. (It's much cheaper, by the way, to buy a share of the company than it is to buy one of its handbags!) If you're more of an athlete than a handbag hound, you can buy shares in Nike. Movie buff? Check out Time Warner's stock price today and see how much it costs to own a little piece of the action. As a shareholder in whatever company stock you buy, you're a mini owner. If the company makes money and the share price goes up, you make money. If it doesn't and the share price declines, you lose money. Simple as that.

You can buy stocks individually or you can buy them within mutual funds, which are "baskets" of multiple individual stocks chosen by a professional money management team. Stock mutual funds, like bond funds, can hold anywhere from thirty or forty individual stocks all the way up to hundreds of them. Unless you have lots of risk tolerance, passion for investing, and time to do research, you're probably better off buying a mutual fund than individual stocks. It's a way to invest in stocks without the pressure of having to research individual companies, stay on top of various industries and investing trends, and eventually make the white-knuckle decisions about if and when to buy and if and when to sell individual stocks. Instead, you buy a mutual fund run by a group of investment professionals who make those decisions for you. Another major advantage of mutual funds is that, because they are composed of multiple stocks, your risk is spread out across multiple companies. If one has a bad year, loses money, or even goes bankrupt, you've got lots of others to potentially fall back on. All of this comes in exchange for a fee, of course, because you're paying the professionals to do the work for you. Most mutual funds charge between 0.2 percent and 2 percent of the total amount you're investing annually, with an average charge of 1.3 percent to 1.5 percent, to run the fund.

Regardless of whether you invest for your long-term financial goals using mutual funds or individual stocks, a common way to gauge the overall performance of the U.S. stock market is by looking at the S&P 500 Index, which is widely accepted in the investment community as a leading indicator of the overall performance of the market. It was established in 1957 and tracks the performance of the five hundred largest stocks traded on the New York Stock Exchange and the NASDAQ stock exchange. Here's the kicker: since 1957, the average annual return of the S&P 500 has been more than 11 percent! This means that, through it all—all the highs and lows—the overall return of all those years averaged together is 11 percent. That includes, of course, the Great Recession. It includes years in which wars have been waged, government corruption has been exposed, unemployment has run rampant, and other huge problems have revealed themselves. (Which, if we think about it, is really every year.) In spite of all that, the number is still 11 percent.

Still nervous? We still understand. Here's an analogy for thinking about the market that might help you feel more comfortable.

The Market as a Picture Window

Imagine that you have one enormous plate-glass window in your living room. Now imagine that the kids in your neighborhood are playing baseball and one of them hits a foul ball straight through your beautiful window. A three-inch hole would destroy the entire thing, and it would require money, as well as a good part of your weekend, to replace it. Not fun. But what if, when you go to repair the window, you do something a bit different. Instead of replacing it with one huge pane of glass the way it was before, this time you replace it with multiple individual window panes. Now the next time a kid (inevitably) hits a foul ball through your window, only one pane is damaged. It's still not optimal, but it's a lot less of a problem than it was the first time, and it costs much less money and time to fix. The risks are lessened.

The same can be true of investing—it's called style diversification, and it can work the same way the paned window does. Investments can be grouped into broad categories that historically have tended to perform differently from one another in any given year. Therefore, if you're invested in a category that performs poorly in a particular year—let's think of that as a window pane breaking—it's unlikely to crash your entire plan. Why? Because there's a good chance that at least some of the other categories will show a positive return that same year—the window panes will remain intact. This isn't a guarantee. Occasionally a terrible storm comes along that might damage all of the panes. But historically speaking, this strategy would help cushion the blow most of the time.

Let's take a look at eight of these broad investment categories, or "window panes," that you might consider investing in for your long-term goals.

Isn't Small Cap a Type of Punctuation?
Understanding Basic Categories of Investments

• Small caps: This refers to stocks issued by relatively small companies. "Cap" stands for "capitalization," which is the total value of the shares of stock issued by a company, so it's equal to the stock price multiplied by the number of shares. For example, if a company has stock worth $100 a share and it issues 2.5 million shares, the capitalization of the company would be $250 million. Now, "small" is a relative term in this context—we're not talking about lemonade stands here. Generally companies in this category have a market capitalization of $250 million to $2 billion, with an average of $500 million. This particular category is tracked by a company called Russell and released as an index called the Russell 2000 Index. It tracks the performance of stocks issued by two thousand small cap companies and calculates an average for all of them. So when people say something like "Small caps are doing well" or "Large caps are doing poorly," they're typically referring to an entire category as tracked by an index; they're not referring to specific individual stocks or mutual funds.

• Mid caps: As you might guess, this category is made up of stocks issued by medium, or "mid"-sized, companies. Companies that fall into this category have market capitalization between $2 billion and $10 billion. The returns are tracked by Russell in the Russell Midcap Index, which measures the performance of eight hundred different midsized companies.

• Large cap growth: This category refers to companies that have market capitalization over $10 billion and that are expected to grow at a faster pace than the rest of the market, as measured by earnings, estimated value, cash flow, and sales. Technology giants like Apple, Google, and Microsoft are often large cap growth companies, though the category as a whole is made up by companies in all sectors. These returns are measured by the Russell 1000 Growth Index, which tracks the returns of one thousand companies in the category.

• Large cap value: As in large cap growth, companies in this category also have market capitalization over $10 billion, but the distinguishing factor here is that we can think of them as relative bargains. Essentially, these stocks trade below their fundamental, or "intrinsic," value for any number of reasons. The result is an opportunity for investors to potentially profit by buying "on sale." The Russell 1000 Value Index tracks this category by monitoring the returns of one thousand stocks that fit the bill.

• International equity: This refers to stocks issued by foreign (non-U.S.) companies. International equity is measured by the MSCI EAFE Index, which tracks more than nine hundred stocks in developed markets outside the United States and Canada. (EAFE stands for Europe, Australasia, and the Far East.)

• Real estate: This refers to investments in commercial real estate, not to any personal real estate you might own. Investors in this category typically purchase something called "real estate investment trusts" (REITs), which work much like mutual funds. Investors pool their money to invest in commercial real estate and potentially profit from it without having to go out to buy and finance individual properties themselves. The FTSE NAREIT Equity REIT Index monitors this category.

• Commodities: If you saw the 1983 movie *Trading Places* (here we are showing our age again!), you may remember the detailed explanation of commodities given to Eddie Murphy's character having to do with orange juice, coffee, pork bellies, wheat, and gold. Commodities are, as the movie suggests, physical substances, such as precious metals, raw materials, grains, meat, oil, and gas. The S&P GSCI Index tracks commodities' performance.

• Fixed income: This is simply another name for bonds, which, as you know by now, are loans to corporations, governments, and other institutions. Fixed-income returns are measured by the Barclays Capital U.S. Aggregate Index. Even though we talked about bonds in the section on short-term goals, we're including them here too because people often invest in them as a way to counterbalance their stock holdings and keep their overall portfolios from becoming too risky. How does that work? Well, this category historically has not returned as much money as the other categories, nor has it lost as much money as the others.

Using the Categories to Your Advantage

Now that we know what we're looking at, what do we do with all this information? Though there are never any guarantees for the future when it comes to investing, from a historical perspective, if you would have spread your investments out across these different categories in any given year, you would have done two things:

1. You would have increased your chances of making money.
2. You would have decreased your chances of losing it.

How? For starters, there has *never* been a year, starting in 1980 all the way through 2013, when all of the "windows broke"—that is, when all categories lost money. (We picked 1980 because not all of the indexes we've mentioned were established before then.) We came darn close in 2008, when all the windows broke except for fixed income, but that one remained intact and showed a positive return. (And in 2009, every single one of them remained intact and showed a positive return!) In fact, in the entire thirty-four-year period from 1980 to 2013 there were only six years when half or more of the windows broke. (In case you're wondering, those years were 1990, 1994, 2001, 2002, 2008, and 2011.) But for the rest of that time period, twenty-eight out of thirty-four years, the majority of windows remained intact. So if your money had been spread out across these categories over the last thirty-four years, you would have improved your chances that at least some of your money would be in an intact window, and therefore would have reduced your risk. With all the drama and fear out there surrounding investing in the market, it's helpful to take a big-picture look at this.

By the same token, no one can ever predict which category will earn the most money in any given year. No single category remained a top performer for more than four consecutive years in our thirty-four-year period, and that happened only once, when international equity was the number one category between 1985 and 1988. More often than not, the top-performing category stayed that way for only a year or two—and it wasn't unusual for the top performer one year to fall all the way to the bottom the very next year. Furthermore, the returns in all eight of these categories ranged from 69 percent to 46 percent in the thirty-four years that we looked at them—a big spread! So how do you know where the best place to invest is? The answer is, you don't! No one does. Historically, if your goal was to increase your chances of making money, you would have spread it out across the categories—which would have given you the chance to keep at least part of your money invested in a positive category, or unbroken window, in any given year. Again, there are no guarantees this will work in the future, but history can provide us with some perspective and comfort as we look at the big market picture.

All of this is known as asset allocation, or sometimes as diversification. These are terms you've probably heard before. Both refer to spreading your money out across these broad categories, yet there is often confusion around this. Diversification does not refer to spreading your money out over different investment companies, financial advisors, or banks. It refers to spreading it across these broad groupings of investments.

Looking at investing in this manner really takes the pressure off, preventing you from thinking that if only you tried harder, you could be savvy enough to know exactly when to get in and out of different types of investments. The reality is, there is no way to predict that. You may be thinking, "Now wait a minute. Surely *someone* has an idea of what's best to invest in now—what about all those swaggering Wall Street geniuses?" Well, despite all the provocative headlines and shrieking voices on television, they don't know either. No one does! That's why diversification has been such a sound investment strategy.

What Does This Have to Do with Building a Portfolio?

Clearly it's important to spread your money out across various categories of investments. But how do we actually do that? Here's how you might use this information to purchase your own combination of stocks, bonds, mutual funds, or similar products, commonly called an investment portfolio. There are almost infinite variations on how you could build a portfolio. Not only do you want to consider what's happening in the investment environment, but also your own personal situation, your objectives, and your risk comfort level to help you create a portfolio that's a good fit for you. If investing and portfolio construction isn't something that you're comfortable with, or if it doesn't sound like your idea of a good time, we suggest you get professional advice. (See Chapter Four for information on how to hire a financial advisor.)

In the meantime, let's look at three basic approaches, just to give you a general idea of how it can work.

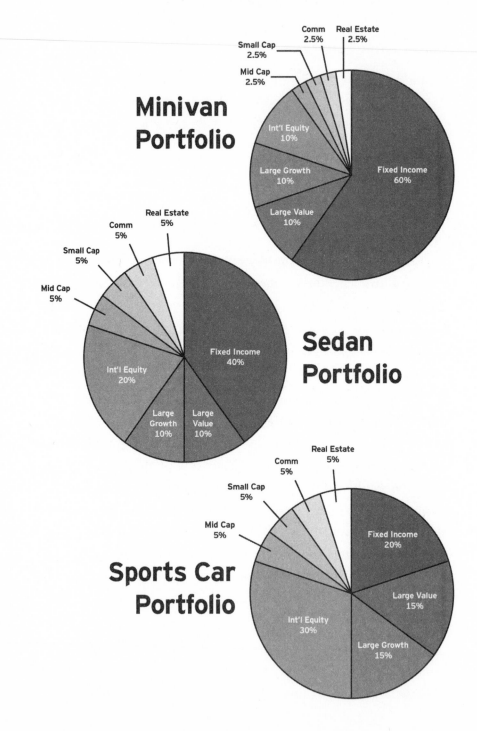

Minivan Portfolio

Comm 2.5%
Real Estate 2.5%
Small Cap 2.5%
Mid Cap 2.5%
Int'l Equity 10%
Large Growth 10%
Large Value 10%
Fixed Income 60%

Sedan Portfolio

Real Estate 5%
Comm 5%
Small Cap 5%
Mid Cap 5%
Int'l Equity 20%
Large Growth 10%
Large Value 10%
Fixed Income 40%

Sports Car Portfolio

Real Estate 5%
Comm 5%
Small Cap 5%
Mid Cap 5%
Int'l Equity 30%
Large Growth 15%
Large Value 15%
Fixed Income 20%

Example One: The Minivan Approach

How have you been feeling as you read this? If you don't think you can stomach opening an investment statement and seeing a big swing in the value of your account, if you are investing for a goal that is less than five to seven years away, or if one of your primary goals is to pull regular income from your investment portfolio, you may want to take a more cautious approach to your investments. Let's call this the "Minivan Approach." This is one way (among many) to invest a significant portion of your portfolio into relatively stable categories, meaning those that have historically shown neither super high nor super low returns. Fixed-income investments have fit that bill very well in the past. Typically, these investments have less upside growth potential, but also less volatility than more growth-oriented investments. In the thirty-four-year period beginning in 1980, the fixed-income category (as measured by the index we mentioned above) had two years of relatively high returns. It returned 32.6 percent in 1982 and 22.1 percent in 1985, but other than those two years, it never topped 18.5 percent, and the lowest return over the whole time period was −2.9 percent. That may seem like a pretty wide range of returns at first, but try comparing it with the international equity category. That category returned a high of 69.4 percent and a low of −43.4 percent in the same time frame. Big difference, right? So, historically, Minivan investors would have done well to put 50 to 60 percent or more of their money into fixed income. (Take a look at the illustration on page 100 for a visual.)

But remember: the point of asset allocation is to spread your money out across categories so that you can potentially increase your chances of making money, decrease your chances of losing it, and keep pace with inflation. Given that, Minivan investors might consider investing a portion—say, 30 percent—of their money in a couple of the more growth-oriented categories, such as international equity with it's thirty-four-year high of 69.4 percent, or in large cap growth and large cap value, which showed highs, respectively, of 41.3 percent and 38.4 percent and lows of −38.4 percent and −36.8 percent over the same thirty-four-year period. The rest of the Minivan portfolio (10 to 20 percent) can be evenly spread across mid cap, small cap, commodities, and real estate. Now your investment portfolio is diversified. Remember, there are infinite approaches you could take to building this kind of portfolio, and this is just one example.

If any of the following statements apply to you, the Minivan Approach might be a good fit:

- You want to see *some* growth for your money, but you don't necessarily need to see *huge* growth.
- You're more concerned about minimizing risk than you are about maximizing gain.
- Your future income stream is limited and you may need to rely on your portfolio within the next five to seven years to supplement your income.
- You're going to need to use this money in the next five to seven years, but you are willing to take some risk in the hopes of seeing some growth with your money.
- You're new to investing, aren't sure what your true appetite for risk is, or want to dip your toe in the investing waters before you dive in.

Example Two: The Sedan Approach

If you would like to see a bit more growth in your portfolio and are willing to take some additional risk in the hopes of making that happen, you may want to take what we have dubbed the "Sedan Approach." As with the Minivan investor, it would make sense for you also to invest a significant amount into the fixed-income category, which has historically shown lower levels of both upside potential for return and downside potential for loss. However, you might be better off limiting your fixed investment portion to 40 percent, as opposed to the Minivan investor's 50 to 60 percent. To give yourself the opportunity for additional potential growth, you would likely want to invest more in the higher risk/higher reward categories of large cap and international equity—say, 40 percent of your overall portfolio, which would leave you about 20 percent to spread across the other categories.

If any of the following statements apply to you, the Sedan Approach might be a good fit:

- You're evenly focused on minimizing risk and maximizing gain.
- You know you get nervous when you see your investment value go down, but you also know you need to invest for growth to meet your long-term goals.
- You anticipate that you will have an ongoing and possibly increasing income stream for at least the next ten years and you feel comfortable that if your portfolio lost money, you would have time to wait for possible market improvement and potentially rebuild it before you need to use it to supplement your income.

Example Three: The Sports Car Approach

Some investors just want to do everything they can to potentially create growth as fast as they can—risk be damned. Well, maybe not damned, but definitely not worried about in the same way as other investors. If you're excited about the possibility of growing your portfolio as much as possible over the long term and you feel comfortable taking the risk that you might experience significant decreases in your investment values at points along the way, the Sports Car Approach may be right for you. Your portfolio would look very different from the previous two. We would suggest you invest only 10 to 20 percent of your portfolio into the lower risk/lower reward fixed-income category. Almost 60 to 70 percent of your portfolio would go into the higher risk/higher reward categories of large cap and international equity. The remaining 10 to 20 percent of your portfolio can be spread across the remaining categories.

If any of the following statements apply to you, a Sports Car Approach might be a good fit:

- Your main objective is to grow your money as much as possible and you're very comfortable taking the risk that you might experience significant volatility along the way in order to get there.
- You're more focused on maximizing gain than minimizing loss.
- You are young and have time on your investing side—you are not likely to need to use this money for many years and you want to see it grow for you.
- You anticipate you will have an ongoing and possibly increasing income stream for decades to come and you feel

comfortable that in the event of a significant portfolio loss, you would have time to wait for possible market improvement and potentially rebuild your portfolio before you need to use it to supplement your income.

You can see that these three approaches are very different from one another, and, again, there are almost infinite possibilities for how portfolios within these approaches can be built. There are also lots of variations on the approaches themselves—maybe you're somewhere between a Minivan and a Sports Car investor. Or maybe you're willing to take even less risk than our Minivan investor. Everyone is different and there are lots of directions any of us could go when making these decisions. That's why we believe working with trained financial advisors is a good idea. They can help you work through the variables and craft an approach that's best for you. We hope the basic investing ideas we've shared here will at least get your wheels turning.

Before we leave this topic, let's go back to Mary one last time. She has identified one long-term goal to focus on from her Prosperity Picture—her nephew Arthur's college fund, which she won't need to access for fourteen years. A great option for her to pursue this goal would be a portfolio that looks a lot like the Sports Car Approach. She would love to see some growth in it for Arthur's sake and she has quite a bit of time before she'll need to access it, so she can potentially rebuild in the event of a loss. When she's ready, she should consider investing about 60 percent of her money into large cap and foreign stock, putting about 10 percent into fixed income, and spreading the remainder across the other categories. Once she initially creates this portfolio, she can set it up to be automatically funded from her checking account so that she doesn't have to remember to do it. She might also consider investing Arthur's college fund using a 529 plan, which is a state-sponsored college savings plan to be used specifically for education and which often provides tax-free growth on earnings in the account. (See Chapter Four for more on this.) No matter how she decides to do it, we think Arthur is one lucky kid!

When Investing, Let Your Stomach Be Your Guide

In the discussion of various investment approaches above, we mentioned risk a lot. Let's talk more about what we mean. Have you ever had a feeling in the pit of your stomach guiding you to do something—or, more likely, *not* to do something? Do you trust this feeling, or ignore your inner guidance system? When it comes to your comfort with investment risk and making investment decisions, we see your gut as a good thing to pay attention to.

Imagine two different routes to get from home to your grandmother's house. You could take the mountain pass or the country road. The pass is a shorter distance and takes less time, but it has steep inclines and sharp turns—clearly a more treacherous ride in bad weather. The country road will take you a lot longer, but is safer. When you think about your investment portfolio, are you planning on taking the mountain pass or the country road? On a sunny day the mountain pass may be a great option, just as a "pedal to the metal" type of portfolio might be when the markets are going up. When it gets dark and the roads are icy, though, this pass might be too frightening for you. Or maybe as long as you have an all-wheel-drive car with traction control, you'll feel safe enough on those more challenging roads and be willing to give it a go.

Just as there are options to get to your grandmother's house, there are choices on the investment routes you take to reach your financial goals. Market ups and downs are the real test of your risk tolerance. If a significant portion of your portfolio climbed to a 38 percent return one year and dropped by 22 percent two years later—not an unusual scenario in volatile periods—how would you feel? This is a very personal question, and one you need to think about carefully. If you're like most people, the pain of losing money is much more intense than the pleasure of making money. This is an instinct so primal we can even see it in monkeys! Researchers conducted a study in which monkeys were allowed to trade tokens for grapes. They observed that when the monkeys didn't get as many grapes as they had been trained to expect, they displayed a very high level of agitation. When the opposite occurred and the monkeys got extra—unexpected—grapes, they showed some happiness, but their happiness appeared to be much less intense than the agitation they showed at loss. Though we may not get quite that emotional about grapes (now chocolate, on the other hand . . .), we can and do show these same kinds of reactions about our investments. It's a phenomenon we don't typically realize until we see our account values decline.

As humans, we hopefully act more rationally than our monkey friends. But because we still have hardwired instincts that can cause us to act irrationally sometimes, it's a good idea to set up your investment portfolio to temper those instincts. If you structure your investments so they're aligned with your risk comfort level *before* the markets decline, you're more likely to be able to balance your emotions with logic and avoid potentially harmful selling at the bottom. Let's say your gut tells you the Minivan Approach seems most comfortable, but you talk yourself into more of a Sedan portfolio so you can potentially earn higher returns. It might be exciting for a while, but what happens when the market inevitably hits a rough patch? Let's go back to the example above of an investment moving from a positive 38 percent return to a negative 22 percent return two years later. If that happened to a significant part of your portfolio, what do you think you would do? If you think you might very well tell yourself, "Enough is enough—I can't afford to lose anymore," and sell those investments at a loss, chances are you would hurt yourself in the long run because you're likely then to miss any potential market recovery. This happens every day, and it's exacerbated when people are invested in securities beyond their comfort level. Be honest with yourself. You'll be much happier, and frankly even healthier, because you can then design your investment portfolio in a way that matches your comfort level with risk.

To help feel more comfortable riding out market downturns, consider establishing a large enough cash cushion (an emergency reserve) to provide you with the money that you might need until the market comes back. Avoid investing money in the stock market that you'll need to use within the next three to five years. If you do invest, and you need to access that money during a bad market, you run the risk of having to sell when your investments are down. The amount to set aside will depend on what's going on in your life over the next three to five years. For example, if you have a child going off to college next year and need to come up with a tuition check, make sure you have that money put aside in a stable, easily accessible account, such as a savings account. If you're retired, consider having enough of your money in cash or in very conservative investments to cover your expenses for one to three years. This will also act as a cushion if you lose your job or have an unexpected need for a large sum of money. If you have enough reserves on the sidelines to cover these kinds of expenses, it can provide you with a greater sense of peace and a lesser chance of freaking out and selling your investments at a bad time based upon fear.

You've likely heard the expression "buy low and sell high." If this were easy to do, we probably wouldn't even have this adage. When markets decline, it can feel as if you're riding a roller coaster. Now, you might be like Ellen and absolutely hate roller-coaster rides. The last roller coaster she rode was the Tidal Wave at Great America. She waited in line for almost an hour for a four-minute ride that resulted in her husband Steven's throwing his back out (later requiring surgery) and her being nauseous for the rest of the day! Now she avoids roller coasters at all costs; the risk, real or not, feels too great. Lisa, on the other hand, loves them. They remind her of her childhood. She feels excited anticipation on the slow ride up and then exhilaration on the fast, steep way down.

Who's right . . . Ellen or Lisa? Well, neither is—or both are. They just have different appetites for roller coasters. Determining the right amount of risk to take with your investments is similar. When you design your investment portfolios, make sure you become deeply in tune with your appetite for risk.

So How Do I Actually Buy This Stuff?

If you don't already have a portfolio, the next logical question is: how do I build one? Within each investment category, there are literally thousands of "products" available.

There are two ways you can buy them. Those of you who already work with an advisor know the first way is to hire a financial advisor who will help you pick the best products for your specific situation and purchase them for you in exchange for a fee or commission. The second way to purchase investment products is to research and buy them yourself. In this case, you obviously need to make the selections on your own. Morningstar.com is a well-regarded independent investment research company and a great place to explore specific investment options; basic membership is free. Once you have an idea of the security you might want to buy and are ready to conduct the transaction, you can do so through an online service. Check out Barron's online (Barrons.com) to find its most recent list of the best online brokers. Make sure to read the fine print before you invest and that you are clear on all the associated costs.

We've covered a lot of critical ideas in this chapter, so let's do a quick recap. We explored practical ways to begin working toward some of the individual goals on your Prosperity Picture. We looked at the basics of investing and the overall performance of different categories of investments. We talked about different approaches to building investment portfolios, the importance of understanding your personal risk comfort, and basic options for purchasing investments. And now we're going to look at techniques you can use to make all this stuff really happen for you!

Gain Traction Through Action

• Review the compound interest chart—bathe in the glory of compound interest!

• Select an image from the "Sooner/More Money" section of your Prosperity Picture. Answer the Picture Planning questions and note your responses in your Prosperity Notebook. Continue this process with other images on your Prosperity Picture.

• Review your current investment portfolio allocations. Are they in line with your goals?

• Do a "gut check" on the risk in your portfolio. Are you comfortable with the amount of risk in your investments? Do you need to learn more about your holdings to feel more comfortable, or do you need to make changes?

Chapter Four

Step Four:
Make It Happen

If all it took was knowledge and a plan, everyone would be in perfect shape and our closets would be totally organized. Our living rooms would look like those annoyingly perfect catalog pages with baskets of fresh flowers and delightful curios placed in artful places. And, of course, our financial households would be in perfect order too. But it takes more than that. It takes action to turn your Prosperity Picture from a pretty collage reflecting your vision to actual results in your life. This doesn't have to be difficult if you are clear on the right actions to take. It's also essential to have the right support along the way—both from within yourself, through strong and positive inner resolve, and from the team you build around you. The right actions often become clear as you examine each goal and become easier to take as you set up systems to stay on track.

So how do you flip the discipline switch to the "on" position and give yourself the best chance to see results? It starts with some exploration of your inner circuitry. If there is faulty wiring running through our beliefs and thoughts about money, it will be nearly impossible to turn plans into reality. But here's the exciting upside: if our internal wiring is sound, our financial lives can reflect that as well.

Think about someone you know who's really made it happen for himself or herself financially. We think of Monica and her husband Ricky. In their late forties, they've managed to save enough to cover their kids' educations, pay off the mortgage on their home, and still put enough aside to be on track for an early retirement. Were they able to make these things happen solely because they make a lot of money? Well, they do earn good incomes, but we've seen people who earn much more than this couple who haven't come close to hitting those kinds of goals. Is it because Monica and Ricky are super savvy investors who made a fortune from their investments? No, it's not that either. Their secret? It's simple. First they made it a priority to cultivate the right *beliefs* around money and then they committed to a series of very smart financial *actions*. These humble, basic decisions have helped move them toward their goals quickly and successfully. No silver bullet, no Thirty-Day Magic Financial Makeover, no get-rich-quick schemes. We know this may not be the answer you expected, so let's take a closer look at how Monica and Ricky have created a strong financial life while others seem to struggle.

When it comes to their financial actions, they do a lot of things right. They have made saving and investing for future goals a top priority. In terms of current spending, they focus on allocating their money in areas that are most important to them. For example, they have a beautiful home because their living environment is meaningful to them. Experiences with their kids also rank high in importance—they take an amazing trip every few years when they feel they've found the right destination and saved the money for the trip. Conversely, cars are low on their list of priorities, so they both drive practical, moderately priced cars. All of these are smart financial actions. But how about if we go deeper and look at their beliefs? Since they were first married, Monica and Ricky have set up their financial lives in such a way that their money reflects their shared values. This has led them to intentionally cultivate supportive financial *beliefs* that affect their everyday decisions. One of the most important? Monica and Ricky have always believed it's essential to live on less than they earn. Building on that fundamental, grounding belief, they have cultivated other helpful beliefs, such as "It's rewarding to be able to put money away in savings," "We're generally happy with what we have," and "We look for ways to use our money to help our own family and also others, especially those in need." Monica and Ricky intuitively know something that offers the keys to the kingdom to the rest of us: their internal mental architecture has as big or bigger an impact on their financial lives as their external financial plan.

What's Happening Inside Your Bird Suit?

Most people think that to reach their financial goals they need more of these three things: money, knowledge, and discipline. Don't get us wrong—these things certainly help. But there's something even more important to making your goals happen that's not nearly as obvious—and that's a supportive mind-set. This is the all-important driver we all have inside our exterior "costume." Without this, it may be very difficult for you to find true prosperity.

Are you still not quite sure you agree? Let's approach this in a slightly unusual way. Think of your favorite *Sesame Street* character. Ours is sweet Big Bird. Let's use him as an example. We logically know there is a person inside the bird costume. (Should we have given you a spoiler alert for that one?) Yet when we're watching Big Bird, we get lost in the story. He seems real—or at least we don't focus on the fact that there's a person inside. Think of your inner money beliefs as the "person inside" the Big Bird suit, and your external actions and habits as the Big Bird character. The person inside is, of course, really running the show. Big Bird can't make much (actually anything) happen on his own. Yet he seems so real at times. Similarly, our relationship with money is guided by our inner thoughts and beliefs—the "person inside" is making the moves, yet we don't usually pay much attention to that. Instead we focus on external factors, expecting just those to get us the results we're looking for. Both are important, but if we had to choose one over the other, we'd go for solid inner workings over savvy external financial strategies every time! Understanding your own money beliefs can provide simple yet profound insight into how you handle money and make financial decisions. Our beliefs about money are very often so ingrained that they appear to us to be truth, not merely how we see things. Sometimes these beliefs have merit, as we saw with Monica and Ricky. But sometimes they are just wrong and don't serve us at all.

Let's think about this in a broader sense. Think back to something you believed was true as a child, and then as an adult realized wasn't true at all. Embarrassingly, while watching a travel show together, Ellen was made aware by her daughter Amy of a false belief she'd been carrying around for years. The host of the show mentioned driving to Alaska. Here's the conversation they had:

Ellen: "You can't drive to Alaska—it's an island."

Amy: "Are you serious, Mom?"

Ellen: "Well . . . it's always separate on the weather maps!"

Amy: "Yeah, an island with a totally straight line on one side!"

They both started laughing hysterically. Ellen could blame Al

Roker and loads of other meteorologists for her false belief, which she tried to do, but realized that wouldn't make it less ridiculous. Thinking Alaska was an island was just an unconscious idea she'd carried around (and thought of as truth) until it was revealed and examined. Is it possible you have ideas about money you believe are true but really aren't? If you can distinguish the *beliefs* you hold about money from the actual *facts*, you'll give yourself a big gift: the flexibility to consciously focus on viewpoints that are supportive and have the power ultimately to help you make great things happen in your financial life.

Conversely, blindness to your beliefs can lead to living your financial life in ways that may be disconnected to what is really happening. For example, can you imagine feeling poor with $9 million? Joan is a crazy-successful corporate executive who does. She's worked for several different Fortune 500 companies as a chief operating officer. During her career she's received a variety of corporate benefits, including stock options, bonuses, and pension plans. Joan is a disciplined saver and has always lived on substantially less than she earns. By her early sixties she's managed to save almost $9.5 million. On the surface this seems amazing—a perfect financial situation.

Here's the rub: inside her "bird suit," Joan believes that she doesn't have much and she can't retire for years! While this is absolutely not true, for her it seems very real. Her money history plays a part in this financial disconnect. She grew up the second youngest of eight kids, and as a child had limited resources with not much money for extras. Joan has been working since she was fifteen years old, and with lots of discipline and hard work, all of the children in her family managed to go to college, but it took a toll on the family finances. At ninety-two, Joan's mom is living on social security benefits and a small pension with no other assets, and is unwilling to accept support from her kids.

Joan looks at the luxurious lifestyles some of her coworkers have, believing they must have a lot more money than she does to spend the way they do, and how her mom lives, which is not how Joan wants to spend her later years, and translates this into believing she doesn't have enough. She worries about spending and doesn't give as much as she could to charities because she's terrified of not having enough. If Joan wants to turn her Prosperity Picture into reality, money isn't the answer; it's reexamining what she believes about money, supported by a good financial plan. It's moving from a mind-set of mental poverty to mental abundance.

For many people, their mind-set creates problems of a very different sort: problems rooted in the pursuit of immediate gratification rather than fear of the financial future. They have beliefs guiding their day-to-day spending decisions that blind them to the future impact on their financial lives. Rhonda, for example, just loves to spend money on things that seem to make her feel good. There's nothing like a door-buster deal to get her heart singing, at least for a short period of time. The problem is, she is living paycheck to paycheck, carrying increasing credit card balances, and putting herself at needless financial risk with her lavish spending. (Though she rationalizes it's okay because "she gets airline miles"!) So what's going on here? Inside her costume, Rhonda feels her life has been such a struggle that she deserves to "treat herself" by spending money on clothes and items for her home, regardless of her ability to actually afford these things. Rhonda does occasionally think about what her life will be like when she's older, but then quickly decides she'll worry about that later. We're all for buying beautiful things, but not when the purchases come at the cost of potential major stress down the road, or when they provide only a short-lived sense of happiness. Rhonda will continue to sabotage her long-term financial success until she has a reset in her beliefs about current spending.

It's hard to move ahead financially when you're burdened with beliefs inside your bird suit that don't serve you. It's like running a marathon while carrying a seven-year-old who's kicking and screaming the entire race. You might eventually be able to get to the finish line—but not easily.

What do *you* believe about money? Do any of the thoughts below sound familiar?

"I'll never be able to retire."

"I'm so bad with money."

"The markets are really risky."

"*Never* spend principal."

"You can't take it with you."

"Rich people are usually crooks."

"It takes money to make money and I don't have what it takes."

"Money corrupts people."

"If I have a lot of money, I'll make other people feel bad."

"It's better to give than to receive."

As you were reading those, we're guessing a few caused you to think, "But that's really true." You may remember times when these money thoughts have shown up in your life. Now ask yourself this question: "If I didn't believe that particular thought, what might be different in my financial life?" Are you open to the possibility that this belief might be limiting your financial progress in some way?

Can you imagine Serena Williams, one of the best tennis players of all time and the winner of more than $50 million in prize money, saying to herself, "Winning will make other people feel bad?" Or, "I'm really not very good at tennis." Of course not. How successful would she have been if her coach had told her, "You know, Serena, women aren't as strong as men at tennis and your backhand isn't very good." It's no different from winning our financial game. You can have rock-solid financial knowledge, but without a supportive mind-set you're likely to struggle. Even if you manage to get where you want to go, the process will likely be miserable.

Where Do Your Financial Beliefs Come From?

We start to develop our attitudes and beliefs about money at an age much earlier than most of us can imagine. According to Dr. Bruce Lipton in his book *The Biology of Belief*, most of our subconscious beliefs are formed between conception and age six. He further goes on to say that 95 percent of the time we operate from our subconscious and only 5 percent of the time from our conscious mind. Could this be true for money beliefs as well? You bet.

Lisa has a godson named Timmy who is an exceptionally pleasant and cooperative kid. When he was three years old his mom asked him to make his bed, and with big brown eyes, he looked up at her and asked, "Can I get 'monies' if I do that?" That simple little question is evidence of a fairly sophisticated set of beliefs about money for someone who is three! It conveys that, first of all, he knew what "monies" were, even though his parents hadn't yet spent a lot of time talking to him about it at that point in his young life. He believed that money was desirable, something he would like to have, even though he probably wasn't sure exactly what he could do with it. He also believed that you could work to earn money, and even that you might be able to negotiate payment for something when it wasn't initially offered. A lot going on in that three-year old mind. (In case you're wondering, Timmy's mom explained that making his bed was part of his responsibilities and not something he could get monies for!)

So what kinds of beliefs did you form about money during your early years? If 95 percent of the way we deal with money is subconscious, thinking back to what happened when our subconscious ideas were developing certainly deserves our attention! Some of your beliefs may have been formed by what you saw. Kids learn a great deal from observation, not just what they are deliberately taught. In Ellen's home, her architect dad went off to work each day at a business he owned. Her mom was always busy—earning an advanced degree, working a variety of different jobs, and eventually starting a company that gave tours of Chicago. Her mother's endeavors were engaging and kept her busy, but weren't necessarily intended to financially support the family. As an adult, Ellen realized she had internalized this model. As she did some exploration, she found she had a belief that it was "the man's job" to earn the money and, further, that her efforts probably couldn't yield much. Whoa! Immediately she realized this thought was not only detrimental, but also totally ridiculous. At the time, she had already earned her MBA from a top business school and was both a CPA and Certified Financial Planner. Once she became aware that she had this unhelpful, deep-seated, subconscious belief, she was able to easily shift it because it so clearly contradicted her life and truth as an adult. Let's spend some time now exploring what some of your subconscious beliefs might be.

What Do You Believe About Money? A Visualization Exercise

To make your Prosperity Picture happen, self-exploration is as or more important than asset allocation, and for some people it is a lot more interesting. So let's focus more deeply on your beliefs about money and the prosperity patterning you've adopted over the years. Set aside a few uninterrupted minutes to reflect on your money upbringing.

Sit in a comfortable position with your legs and arms uncrossed. Take in a few deep breaths. It might help to breathe in through your nose and out through your mouth. With each inhale and exhale, become more and more relaxed. Take in a few more deep breaths and feel yourself becoming comfortable, calm, and quiet.

Now think back to your early childhood. In your mind's eye, see yourself as a child. Think back to your earliest memory that involved money. Who was with you? What did they say to you? What did you say to them? Where were you when this took place? Remember the feelings you experienced as this happened.

Now recall another memory about money from your childhood. Maybe a little later in your life—perhaps between ages ten and nineteen. Did this incident involve a time you earned money? How often did you talk about money in your home? What kinds of conversations took place about money? Were there feelings of lack? Feelings of plenty or more than enough? Was there calm or was there some turmoil?

What messages are you hearing about money at that age? How is your money personality developing? What is it you are beginning to believe about money?

Now move on to your adult life. Think of one very powerful

money memory. What is this memory? Who is with you? How are you feeling about money? How did your early life bring you to this point in time? What is it you believe to be true about money? Now ask yourself: Do these beliefs serve you? Do they hinder your success?

When you are ready, gently bring your attention back to the present moment. Take some time to write in your Prosperity Notebook about any impressions you have from this visualization. What money beliefs were identified to you? Are these helpful or hindering beliefs?

If you're like most of us, you've discovered some thoughts, attitudes, and beliefs that are helpful and others that are not so much. Often merely uncovering your unsupportive beliefs can help you to shift them. For example, Ellen no longer believes Alaska is an island, nor does she believe that it's the man's job to earn money! Sometimes you might need more support. Later in this chapter we'll share breakthrough strategies for when those sabotaging thoughts show up. Replacing limiting financial beliefs with more supportive ones will help propel you toward your goals and make taking the right actions so much easier.

The Consequences of Negative Thinking

Are limiting financial beliefs really that big a deal when it comes to our money? Absolutely! It can be difficult, if not impossible, to make your plan happen if you don't believe you can do it. Negative thinking can have dire consequences for our wealth and our health. You're probably familiar with the placebo effect—when people experience a positive health improvement from the expectation of a treatment, as opposed to the actual treatment itself. You may be less familiar with something called the "nocebo effect" (*nocebo* means "I will harm" in Latin). Just as positive beliefs about a treatment can heal, negative beliefs that we are susceptible to illness or have been exposed to a toxic substance can make us ill. In one experiment, volunteers were told they would be receiving a mild electric current passing through their heads and it might cause a headache. Although no actual current was used, two thirds of the subjects reported experiencing headaches. Similarly, in an antidepressant drug trial one patient who was given placebo tablets proceeded to take twenty-six tablets in a suicide attempt and ended up in considerable peril. Even though the pills were chemically inert, the participant's blood pressure dropped dangerously low.

How can we apply this idea to helping us realize our financial goals? If our minds can produce these types of dramatic effects in physical situations involving complex biological and chemical realities, imagine how positive and negative beliefs about money can impact financial situations! When we met Cheryl, a successful marketing consultant, the first thing she said to us was, "I'm incompetent when it comes to money. When my husband and I meet with Bob, our financial advisor, the language he uses doesn't land with me at all. I don't follow along very well, so I usually check out. But I did know about two particular stocks that I thought might be good places to invest when the markets were really low. I knew the companies well through work and I also knew the prices were ridiculously low. When I suggested them, my husband and the advisor totally shut down the idea. Since then the stocks have gone up almost 200 percent."

Cheryl didn't sound incompetent to us. She's bright and has a clear understanding of the businesses she was interested in investing in. We weren't there during the conversation, but we're guessing that when she made the suggestion, it was colored by her belief that she's "incompetent" with money. The discussion might have gone as follows:

CHERYL: "I'm not really sure about this, but what do you think about investing in X and Y companies? The stock prices are really low now."

BOB THE ADVISOR: "No, that's not a good idea with the volatility in the markets. The beta on that stock is way too high."

CHERYL: (Thinks to herself: *I wonder what "beta" is? Obviously I don't really know much about this.*) "But it seems like such a good opportunity. At least I think it is."

HUSBAND: (Thinks to himself: *I wonder what "beta" is? Doesn't matter—I know what I'm doing here.*) "Look, no one knows what's going on now. That's a bad move—we should listen to Bob."

CHERYL: (Thinks to herself: *They must know more than me about this, but still . . .*) "Well, okay . . ."

Well, first of all, "beta" is simply a fancy way to refer to volatility in an investment or portfolio compared with the market as a whole.

Second, and more important, Cheryl's limiting thoughts about her financial abilities came through in her communication style as well as in her confidence to move ahead, even when her knowledge and instincts told her it was a good move. With her attention on her financial insecurities, she was easily able to find evidence that her belief was true—that she was "incompetent" when it comes to money. This limiting thought would clearly be an obstacle for Cheryl in making her plan happen.

Betty, on the other hand, keeps her attention on the abundance flowing in her life. She started her life after college as a professional dancer. She loved what she was doing, but after about eight years was looking for her next career move. She started to work part-time at a call center, answering questions and taking orders for an education company. Betty soon realized she could run the operation better, more efficiently, and probably more profitably than her employer. Armed with the right beliefs—she could indeed do this and it was an amazing opportunity—she started her own call center. Within two years the business was bringing in millions of dollars, and within six years she sold it for enough money to give her financial security for the rest of her life. It would be easy for a professional dancer to think, "What do I know about running a business?" Or, "What if this doesn't work out?" But Betty didn't allow herself to have those kinds of thoughts. Instead, she used her belief in the abundance effect to help make her goal a reality.

Think of the abundance effect as the nocebo's good twin. It's all about having positive, prosperous beliefs to support you in reaching your goals. The abundance effect shields you from the limiting beliefs that keep you from being your best, reaching your goals, and enjoying the process.

Moving from Concern to Confidence

If you're more like Cheryl than Betty, how do you move from thoughts of fear and limitation to thoughts of confidence and expansiveness? Try this easy three-step process. Step one is simply to become more aware of your money thoughts. Let's say you receive an investment statement in the mail and catch yourself thinking, "I'm not even going to open this—I'm sure I must have lost money." At that moment, pause. Be aware of the fact that you just had a negative thought. This may sound silly at first—of course you're aware you had the thought; you just had it! But scientists estimate the average number of thoughts we have per day to be up to seventy thousand. That's a lot! So many that it's easy to have negative thoughts and not even pay attention to the fact that we're having them. Hence, awareness has to come first.

Let's say you tell yourself, "Well, I'll never be able to really 'retire' anyway." Step two is deciding whether you like the idea, want to foster it, or want to see it come to fruition. Since we're talking about negative thoughts here, you probably don't like it, so go ahead and call it out as an undesirable thought, which you do not want to encourage or see happen (even though, let's be real, at times it may happen anyway—this isn't magic, just an effective management technique). Just tell yourself, "Of course I don't want that to happen."

Finally, step three is to say to yourself, "cancel/clear." Cancel the thought and clear it away. Sometimes it can be that simple. *Cancel/clear.* At one of our workshops a woman told us she tells herself to "star-seven," which is how she deletes messages from her voice mail. Imagine changing the channel on your TV or skipping to the next song on your playlist.

This easy technique can work wonders. We both tell ourselves to cancel/clear multiple times per day—whenever we have negative thoughts about money or any other issues in life! It makes us feel calmer and happier, and we believe it positions us for success. Try this for a week. Notice each time you have negative money thoughts, consciously decide you do not want these thoughts to happen, and then say to yourself, "cancel/clear." Take a moment to make a hash mark in your Prosperity Notebook to track how often you have negative thoughts. Noting this will help you be more aware and remind you to cancel/clear your negativity away.

One thing to keep in mind here: this technique is most effective for the thousands of fleeting thoughts we have on a daily basis. If a particular negative thought keeps coming up repeatedly, you may need to do some deeper work to eliminate the beliefs. In Chapter Six we'll share with you Dr. Tim Ursiny's Truth Talk strategy. It's easy, quick, and effective.

What Do You *Really* Want? Tactical Approaches to Making It Happen

Now that we've spent some time inside the bird suit and taken a close look at our powerful beliefs about money and how we can harness them to help make things happen in our financial lives, let's consider more external/tactical ways you can bring your Prosperity Picture closer to reality. Take a look now at the images on your Prosperity Picture and the Goals List you created in Chapter Three. Some of these goals will likely be more important to you than others. Yes, of course it would be awesome to see all of them show up in your life. We hope they do! But to start your plan, it helps to rank them in order of how important they truly are to you. For example, you may really like the idea of attending a cooking class in Tuscany, but when you think about it you don't want this more than an opportunity to start your own business. Well, then, saving to start your own business would surely top Tuscany on your priority list.

Take a few minutes right now to prioritize your Goals List in your Prosperity Notebook. From a quiet, relaxed state, tune in to how important each goal truly is to you. For this part, don't worry about *how* you will achieve the goal or even if you believe it's possible to achieve. If you feel conflicted in choosing the priority, ask yourself these questions as you look at each image:

- If I could never achieve this goal, how would I feel?
- Who else will benefit from this goal?
- Is this my goal or actually someone else's goal?
- Does this goal make my heart sing or does it feel like an obligation?

Now rank your Goals List in order of importance, beginning with your number one priority and moving on from there. This ranking will help you allocate your savings toward different goals and also make decisions about how to most effectively invest toward each goal, given the related time frame.

Use the "Financial Flowerpot" System to Help You Reach Your Goals

Whatever your personal goals may be, there are tricks you can use to make saving for them easier. Traditional economics tells us that money is a medium of exchange and that people are *rational* decision makers around money. Rational? Really? We all know this isn't true a good part of the time. People can be really goofy when it comes to money decisions. Behavioral finance is a field of study that embraces the idea that people are sometimes irrational when it comes to money, and understanding the basics of behavioral finance can be helpful in planning.

Behavioral economists have discovered that most people think of their money in separate pools—our retirement money, the kids' education funds, my vacation account, etc. Although your money could be used for almost any purpose, this mental accounting can be quite helpful, because we naturally organize our thinking about finances this way. You can use this notion of mental accounting to your advantage. Here's how: Imagine a row of flowerpots on your windowsill. Each imaginary pot represents an account where you "plant" a goal. When you direct money into this account, it's like watering and feeding your goal.

One of the best ways to fill up those "financial flowerpots" is to establish a regular saving and investing plan, especially if it's structured for your monthly contribution to be automatically withdrawn from a paycheck or a checking or savings account. This makes reaching your goals easier, for a simple reason: most of us do better when things happen automatically. Think of an automatic savings plan working in the same way that an automatic watering system might in an actual flowerpot—you set it up once and it does the work for you, simple as that.

Some of the goals reflected on your Prosperity Picture may initially seem to be unattainable, even pipe dreams. But by developing a systematic plan and funneling your savings into specific financial flowerpots earmarked just for that purpose, you're taking the right steps to turn that pipe dream into a reality. This may happen even more quickly than you think possible.

As we explored in Chapter Three, it's important to match the type of investment you'll use to fill each flowerpot with the timing of your goal. For example, if you're working toward something two years from now, you wouldn't want to choose an investment likely to fluctuate in value, because you'll need to access your funds soon. If you go to get the money and that flowerpot happens to be down in value, you'll be unhappy and you may not have time to wait for it to potentially build up again. A more stable investment probably wouldn't give you as much upside potential, but it might be the better choice for this kind of short-term goal. On the other hand, if you're saving for something fifteen years from now, you might be better off putting the money into an investment with more upside potential, even though it's probably more volatile—you'll have time to ride it out. For a refresher on this, go back and review the section on building a portfolio in Chapter Three (see pages 99–111).

Creating your Goals List in Chapter Three hopefully gave you a good idea of what might belong inside each of your financial flowerpots and now you can begin to prioritize which ones you'll be feeding and watering first. This is a powerful step in making prosperity happen for yourself—and obviously very personal to you. We're going to come back to your personal Prosperity Picture–driven flowerpots shortly, but first we would like to make some suggestions for three more "universal" pots that, if not already on your windowsill, are worthy of consideration.

Three Financial Flowerpots Most People Should Think About

There are three main flowerpots to think about adding to your financial garden—pots so essential for a successful financial future that everyone should, at the very least, give serious consideration to incorporating them in their financial planning.

Your Solutions Flowerpot

This one is a biggie. If you don't already have something like this in place, we recommend that you set up a "solutions flowerpot." *Everyone* who wants to create his or her own prosperity needs one.

This is more commonly referred to as an emergency fund, but we prefer to think of it in terms of solutions because it provides you with a way to solve problems and have a financial cushion in case of unforeseen situations like a job loss, a medical situation not covered by insurance, or an unexpected expense related to your home or car. A cheerier way to look at this is to think of it as a "sunny day" pot—something to give you peace of mind that you have resources in place to provide a solution for you and your loved ones to feel secure, be healthy, and live comfortably even in the face of changing circumstances. It gives you financial flexibility should you need it in the future.

We suggest that you set aside at least six to twelve months of living expenses you can access immediately and without penalty for this purpose. If you or your partner has an unusual job that would be difficult to replicate or if you work in a field where job mobility is limited, you may want to consider increasing your solutions cash reserve to twelve to twenty-four months' expenses. When deciding on how much you should set aside, take into account how much of a cash cushion will help you sleep better at night. Don't underestimate the value of reducing anxiety when it comes to your finances. Less stress leads to better decisions.

You may be thinking, "Six to twelve months of expenses? Are you crazy?" We know it's a lot—we've been there. If it just doesn't seem feasible for you to put aside that much money all at once, start by putting aside something and building as you can. We don't care if it's $5 a week, $50 a week, or $500 a week. The point is to get started.

If this still doesn't seem feasible and you feel like you need a solutions pot for your solutions pot, here's another tactic: if you own your home, see whether you qualify for an equity line of credit against your house. This is a promise from a lender (typically a bank) to let you borrow money now or in the future and pay it back to them at a "favorable" rate, with your house serving as backup or collateral on the loan. In most cases the interest you're charged is tax deductible. This can be a cost-effective way to borrow, but of course this also means that if you need to borrow against your home and don't pay it back, the bank has the right to take your house! So, for obvious reasons, you don't want to fool around with this. Using an equity line of credit is not our first recommendation for your solutions flowerpot, but if it's the only viable option for you, it's better to have it available than not. It's much easier to get one established when you don't actually need it. You don't have to borrow from it now, but the option will be there if you need it down the road. There is usually a small fee for keeping the line open even if you are not using it, but this may be worth the peace of mind it brings.

Your Retirement Flowerpot

Retirement is a hot topic and most people have goals involving it. If you're in a position where you're certain you'll have access to the money you need to live on for the rest of your life, and you don't have any further goals for your retirement, you don't need this pot. If that's not the case for you, you should set up a "retirement flowerpot." How much you'll need to save for your future financial independence will of course depend on a variety of factors. For example, when do you want to retire? Often people say, "Tomorrow!" So maybe we should add *realistically* to that question. Next you'll want to consider how much you'll need to live on when you stop working. This typically isn't an easy question to answer, as you might not know where you'll live or exactly what you'll be doing in retirement. Our suggestion is to start by looking at what you are currently spending and adjust from there. Your retirement spending may be more than your current spending if you plan some major travel, significant continuing education, or other costly activities. On the other hand, it may be less than your current spending if you plan on downsizing and simplifying your life.

Next you'll need the details of future income you'll receive, such as pensions, social security, or potential inheritances. (However, we don't usually encourage counting on an inheritance unless you know it will be large and you're confident your parents or benefactors won't spend it all.) Part of this equation also includes the current amount of money you've put away for retirement, how much you can save between now and then, and assumptions for inflation and the growth on your investments. There are lots of moving pieces for sure—this is not a calculation you can do in your head! Instead, we recommend you use an online retirement calculator or work with a financial planner to help customize projections for your specific situation.

Once you know what you need to save to reach your retirement goal, you can set up automatic investments into your retirement flowerpot. Here are some guidelines on where to allocate your retirement savings, in order of priority:

If you or your partner has a 401(k) or similar employer-sponsored retirement plan available at work, your first retirement planning move should be to do everything you can to contribute the maximum into these plans (the IRS sets limits on how much you can contribute, and your employer may have its own limits). Why? First of all, your employer may match your contributions, often doing so at a percentage of your contribution up to a certain amount. You don't want to miss out on your employer's help in saving for the future. There are also tax benefits to contributing to 401(k), 403(b), and similar plans. The money you put into the plan reduces your taxable income for the year. So, in effect, the government is helping to fund part of the contribution by not taking its bite up front. Any growth of the money contributed to the account will be tax deferred—you won't have to pay taxes on the growth until you take the money out of the plan in retirement. If your company offers a Roth 401(k), the situation is a little different; in this case, the government *does* take its bite, so there's no tax savings now, but when you go to take the money out during retirement, any investment growth will be tax free.

Another reason we recommend you contribute the maximum amount possible into your retirement plan is that the forced savings is usually super supportive in helping people hit their goals. Once you set up your contributions, the money will come out of your paychecks automatically, and most people quickly get accustomed to living without this money. This systematic savings plan acts like a silent coach making sure you put money away for the future.

Here's a little-known 401(k) tip or trap: Our friend Kate was reviewing her 401(k) statements and realized that she had somehow not gotten her full matching contribution from her company even though she had maxed out her personal contributions. She and her financial advisor did some investigation and learned that, in some situations, to qualify for the full company matching, your contributions need to be made in *each pay period* throughout the year. In other words, if you max out your contributions early in the year—say, through a bonus—or if you only contribute for part of the year, you might be leaving some employer matching money on the table. If you're not sure how your company's plan is structured, check with the human resources department or the person in charge of benefits.

If you don't have a retirement plan through work, or if you do and want to sock away even more money, the next type of account to consider is an IRA, or individual retirement account. Think of an IRA as a container that can hold almost any type of investment and allow it to grow, tax deferred, until you take the money out during retirement. This gives you an advantage because it saves you tax money during your earning years and, since the money grows tax free, allows you to potentially build up a bigger pile within your IRA container. Some experts theorize that there may be an additional advantage when you go to withdraw money when you retire because many people drop into a lower tax bracket at that point, since they're no longer earning a salary. This may or may not be the case. It's hard to know for sure, because tax laws can and do change frequently. Regardless, we know we can all enjoy the tax deferral on earnings within an IRA right now, even if things change down the road.

There are several types of IRA—traditional, Roth, SIMPLE (Savings Incentive Match Plan for Employees), and SEP (Simplified Employee Pension). Traditional and Roth IRAs are designed for individuals, while SEP IRAs and SIMPLE IRAs are meant for self-employed people and small businesses. The eligibility requirements and contribution limits for the various types change frequently, and a good way to stay on top of them is to check out the IRS Web site: www.irs.gov/Retirement-Plans/Individual-Retirement-Arrangements-(IRAs)-1. Or check with your financial advisor or CPA for advice.

Your College Flowerpot

If you have kids you want to send to college and that goal isn't already one of the flowerpots in your garden, you will want to make it one. If you are planning on paying for college for your children, in part or in full, our best advice is to start early. With time on your side, you'll be more likely to be able to amass enough money to cover the crazy cost of higher education. If you are even *thinking* about having kids, start saving. How much do you need to save? This will depend upon the type of education you want to fund—private or public university, for example—the age of your kids, your savings ability, as well as the possibility of scholarships or grants. There are online financial calculators to help in this process. If you haven't started to save and your children are older, there's still some time to catch up. The important thing is to start.

Where should you save this money? Consider a 529 college savings plan. These are tax-advantaged savings plans sponsored by states, state agencies, and educational institutions and authorized by Section 529 of the Internal Revenue Code. There are two different types of 529 plans. One is a prepaid tuition plan. These state-sponsored plans allow you to purchase credits or units to be used at participating universities at some point in the future; often you need to be a resident of the state sponsoring the plan. The second type of 529 plan is a college savings plan. These are plans that allow an account to be set up to benefit a student and help pay for eligible college education costs. The student can use this money for education costs at any college or university—it doesn't have to be in the state where the plan is established. This second type allows you to choose among investment options. Often there are age-weighted investment options, which are a portfolio of mutual funds that will automatically become more conservatively invested as the child gets closer to college age (to help protect your investment from volatility and improve the chances that it will be there when you need to access it). A big benefit of these types of plans is that when the money is used to pay for higher education costs, any investment earnings are free from federal taxes and most often from state taxes as well. If you use the money for something other than college costs, though, you'll be subject to taxes and penalties, so be careful to avoid overfunding your 529 plans.

What Other Flowerpots Need Watering?

Now that we've covered the Big Three flowerpots, let's go back to your top-priority personal ones from your Goals List. Go ahead and set up separate accounts to save for these goals—name them accordingly, if you wish. Often financial institutions will allow you to set a name or goal to the online profile of an account. If it's a longer-term goal you're investing for, give that a name too. We know a couple who has been saving in their Tahiti account for years, so their financial advisor labeled it "Tahiti account" on their statements. Have fun with this. Making your goals happen shouldn't be all serious business.

A Financial Flowerpot at Work

Let's examine a specific Goals List example. Say the number one priority on your Goals List is a trip to Hawaii and you have made that your first personal flowerpot. If a Hawaii trip costs $8,000, you may initially think, "I can't do this—I need to save for retirement, I've got the kids' college coming up, etc. . . ." You, of course, know that putting this trip on a credit card and worrying about it later is a bad idea. So look at it this way: if you were to save $120 a month (about $30 per week)—even if you just saved it, with no return at all on your investment—you would have $7,200 after five years, almost enough for your vacation! Okay, the price might go up during those five years, but you get the idea. If you were to invest that money and receive a hypothetical average annual return of 3 percent, you would have $7,769 after five years—even closer to your vacation. And if you were to receive a hypothetical average annual return of 5 percent, you would have $8,171—enough for the vacation plus some nice souvenirs.

If we put into historical context these possible rates of return for our hypothetical Hawaii trip, they would have been quite reasonable expectations—remember, the annual return of the S&P 500 since its inception has averaged more than 11 percent. Be aware that the rates of return are purely hypothetical—there's no guarantee you would get them. But you can see the potential that's out there.

Feel Like You Can't Afford to Save?

By now you might be thinking, "This all sounds great, but I just don't have extra money to save." When you start a savings plan—even if it's for a very exciting reason, like a Hawaii trip—it can feel like you're losing money. And we all hate to lose money.

But here's an interesting phenomenon to consider. In a public opinion survey, half of the people surveyed were asked whether they thought they could save 20 percent of their income. Only half of this group said yes. When the other half of the people surveyed were asked whether they thought they could live on 80 percent of their income, almost 80 percent said yes. To *save* 20 percent of your income is exactly the same as *living* on 80 percent of it. So these results don't make any logical sense. But it makes intuitive sense because of the way many of us view money. To redirect 20 percent of your cash flow into savings somehow feels as though you're losing it. Living on 80 percent of your income may be an initial adjustment, but ultimately doesn't seem so much like a loss—it's simply what is available, and focuses on what you do have, not on what you don't have. It's all about how you look at it! So if your plan shows that you should be saving and investing 18 percent of your income and you initially think you can't do it, try thinking of it instead as having 82 percent of your income available to you.

Still think it sounds hard to save? This is an opportunity to check in on your thoughts, attitudes, and beliefs about your money. Setting up an automatic savings plan for a goal you're jazzed about might be just the thing to make the belief "It's so hard to save" switch to "It's so fun to save!"

How does that sound? If you're still not buying it and believe you can't save what you need in order to reach your goals, try to cancel/clear that thought away. Still not working? Maybe then it's time to take another look at your goal and decide how truly important it is to you. There might be a conflicting goal that is actually more important.

Build Your Personal Support Team

One of the best ways to make your financial goals happen is to set up the right support team—both personal and professional. We're generally not very good at getting support around our money goals. People tend to be super secretive when it comes to anything related to personal finances. Most people reveal the details of their financial life only to a very select group of people, if at all. But you really don't have to fly solo to meet your Prosperity Picture goals. It can be so much more difficult to reach your goals if you don't get support, encouragement, and input from others. It's similar to creating a fitness goal and deciding to work out with a friend, take a group class, or hire a personal trainer. Having supportive people around you can help you reach your goals much more efficiently. If you're a bit uneasy about this, remember you don't need to share all the gory details and specific numbers to have your friends and family support you. Letting them know your general goals can be just fine, and you can still benefit from their encouragement and insight.

Having said this, we caution you to be careful who you choose to be on your team. Getting the right type of help from the right people is also crucial. Ever have a goal you were really excited about, only to have it shot down by someone? This someone might even be a person who loves and cares about you. Sometimes our goals are not the same or may conflict with our loved ones' goals. Silvia knows this firsthand. Her parents worked very hard to get her through college and medical school and were incredibly proud of their daughter when she became an ER doctor. Silvia had a secure job at a local hospital and made very good money. There was only one problem. She hated her work. Silvia was stressed, miserable, and searching for ways to live her passion—which was theater. She loved acting, writing, and directing. She searched desperately for ways to incorporate this into her life. Any time she broached this subject with her parents, she was met with confusion and anger. How could their brilliant daughter think of doing anything but being a respected physician? Silvia realized that, as close as she felt to her parents, they were not the people she needed to support her for this goal. She found a trusted theater friend as well as a good financial advisor to help her figure out how to practice medicine less and do more theater work. Fast-forward five years—Silvia is now working part-time in a clinic and running a small theater company. No, she's not making as much money as before, but she loves her life. Be discriminating when you choose the team to help you along the way. This safety tip could apply to friends, professional advisors, coaches, or even your spouse or partner.

Professional Guidance to Make It Happen: Hire a Financial Advisor or Do It Yourself?

Once you get your personal team in place, the next step is to think about professional guidance. If you don't already have one, you need to decide whether you should hire a professional financial advisor. This decision begins with self-examination. Take a moment to go through the following statements, answering yes or no for each one.

1. I enjoy researching new investment topics.
2. I feel excited when I figure out a financial problem on my own.
3. I enjoy analyzing financial details.

4. I hate paying for services I can do myself.

5. I am fascinated by how the markets work.

6. I understand how to use online calculators (or I'm confident I can learn) to help me know whether I am on track for my goals.

7. I am confident in my ability to choose investment vehicles, to create a well-diversified portfolio, and to monitor a portfolio.

8. I need and want professional advice to create an investment portfolio and monitor my investments on an ongoing basis.

9. I want a professional to help me know whether I am on track for my goals.

10. I am happy to pay for advice when it saves me time.

11. I am happy to pay for advice when it saves me money.

12. I think having a professional will make discussions about money easier for me and my partner.

13. Although I'm comfortable managing my own money, my partner is not. I want someone for him/her to work with if something happens to me.

14. I believe most vetted professionals are basically trustworthy.

If it's not already clear to you, your answers to these questions can help you decide whether you want to handle your money questions, issues, planning, and investing on your own, or whether it makes more sense to hire an expert to walk you through this process. If you had more yeses than noes on questions 1 through 7, you may be well suited to handling your money and investments on your own or with only a limited amount of professional assistance. If you had more yeses than noes on questions 8 through 14, then hiring a financial advisor might be the way for you to go.

As you make this decision, also consider the fact that just because you *can* do something on your own doesn't always mean you *should*. Think about fixing and maintaining your car. Maybe adding washer fluid is simple, but changing the oil is too hard. Or maybe you can change the oil or fix a flat tire, but for anything else the car goes to the shop. It's not that you couldn't learn to do more complicated repairs, but you might not have the time, the interest, or the patience to learn. Should you spend the time to find a trustworthy mechanic? Of course you should. Should you understand enough to make sure you aren't overpaying or getting bad advice? Certainly. And if you think it's fun and you have the knowledge to work on your own car, then by all means you should do so—but it's not for everyone. Similarly, we believe that working with a qualified financial advisor can be a smart money move for many people.

How to Hire a Financial Advisor

If you decide you want to work with a financial advisor, the next step is figuring out how to choose the right one for you and your situation. The best way to do that is to clarify for yourself what you want your advisor to do for you.

Are you like Jolene, who loves doing her own investing, researching investment alternatives and working through financial strategies, but doesn't feel comfortable totally flying on her own? Jolene wants to have a professional to bounce ideas off, check in on her investment allocations, and help her with retirement projections. She decided to work with a financial planner who will charge her a fee for general advice.

Or are you more like Brenda? Brenda was originally looking to hire an advisor after her divorce. She knew she needed to learn more about how to handle her money and was concerned about her financial security. She found a financial advisor who looked at her entire financial life, talked about her future plans, and helped Brenda to feel confident that she would be on track with her goals. Brenda's advisor also helped her to invest and monitor her investments on an ongoing basis. Brenda paid a fee for the financial planning and a percentage of her investments for ongoing management.

Perhaps you're more like Janet and Ty. They are both involved with managing the family finances, but are also really busy with two small children. They decided they wanted to work with an advisor who would help them understand their insurance needs, plan for educating their two children, and at the same time plan for their retirement. They were referred to an advisor who gets paid based solely upon the commissions she earns on the investments she helps Janet and Ty make.

There are a variety of ways these advisors get compensated for the work they do. We don't believe there is one best way. We do know it's crucial that you understand how you are being charged, that you're clear on what you can expect from your advisor, and that you feel very comfortable with him or her. You'll be baring your financial soul to your advisor, so you need to make sure you're good with that. Most people don't share such information with anyone else other than their partner and maybe their accountant or attorney.

We suggest you approach this in the same way you would if you were looking for a new doctor. Instead of finding a specialist for your medical condition, you're searching for a person to help with your wealth health. You might get a referral from a friend who's had a great experience, another professional, or a professional association (see the "Gain Traction Through Action" section at the end of this chapter for a listing of professional organizations for financial advisors). Think through whether you need someone who has a particular specialty (such as expertise in the divorce process, special-needs kids, or business succession planning). When you first meet them, sit back and relax. Think about whether you're comfortable with their approach, philosophy, and service model. And as you might with a doctor, think about how comfortable you are with their "bedside manner." Make sure the advisor is easy to talk to and that you feel a real sense of trust. You can also double-check to see whether your potential advisor has any complaints against him or her by going to FINRA BrokerCheck, a site designed for investors to research brokerage firms, brokers, and investment advisors. (www.finra.org/Investors/ToolsCalculators/BrokerCheck).

It's also helpful to ask a prospective advisor about his or her typical clients—how old they are, what goals they're planning for, and the size of their investment portfolios, for example. Also, make sure to understand whether the advisor requires a minimum amount of money to be invested in order to work with them. You'll want to make sure your situation matches their expertise. If they deal only with multimillionaires and you are just starting out, you might not get the attention you are looking for. On the other hand, don't assume you "don't have enough" money to invest in order to work with a professional advisor. Financial advisors all work differently, and the best way to learn about one in particular is simply to ask questions up front, including what their minimum levels of investment are.

Part of a Couple? Make Sure You're on Each Other's Support Team

If you have a significant other, working closely with that person is another great way to make your hopes and dreams happen. It seems like an obvious point, but quite often couples don't communicate openly about their financial situation. They may avoid the topic or keep secrets from each other, fearing such discussion will lead to arguments. At a dinner we hosted, one young woman told a story about how her mom routinely hides shopping bags in the trunk of her car until she can sneak them into the house without her husband seeing them. Such scenarios are not uncommon. But if you work with your partner to communicate openly about money and create a shared financial vision, you will build a strong and resilient foundation for both your money and your life.

We typically see that in most couples, financial responsibilities are delegated to one person. That is 100 percent fine, with one important caveat: both people need to be aware of the basics of their financial situation. You both need to be aligned on your general financial approach. And you both need to know the details of where your accounts are, how to access them, and where your key documents are. This is nonnegotiable. If we were talking about your physical health instead, this would be like both of you needing to get an annual checkup, ensure that your blood pressure is stable, and check that you have healthy cholesterol levels. You would also both ideally want to have similar ideas about your general health and wellness approach. And, of course, you would both need to know where your doctor's office is located, where the insurance cards are stored, and how you can access your past medical records. These are the basics.

Barbara, one of our workshop attendees, said that because her husband is an accountant and her interests are more creative, she really had no knowledge of the details of their financial life. Her husband told her that if anything happened to him suddenly she should call his partner Larry, and he would help. Initially Barbara was comforted knowing she had someone she could lean on in an emergency, but realized after attending the workshop that she needed to take a more active role to ensure her long-term financial security. So she set up a series of meetings with her husband to make sure she knows the details of their financial situation, where the important documents are, and what she would do if he were to die before her. She will still get Larry's help if her husband passes away before her, but she'll be much more knowledgeable about their situation.

Understand the Basics as a Couple

To start tackling the financial basics as part of a couple, channel your inner Girl or Boy Scout. Make sure you're both prepared for the unexpected by knowing the most basic details of your shared financial lives. The last thing you want to worry about in a difficult scenario is what the password is for your online bank accounts, yet you may find yourself doing just that if you don't gather this information in advance. This is an easy one—it shouldn't take any more than an hour to go through these questions together. Make sure both of you know the following:

- The exact location of all key financial documents (see chapter appendix for a list).

- Contact information for all key professional partners: financial advisor, accountant, attorney, insurance agents, and any others who support you.
- Account passwords for all online financial accounts.
- Safe-deposit box information. Do you have one? If so, do you both know where the key is?

The Major Financial Building Blocks for Couples

Next, make sure you're on the same page for each of the foundational building blocks of your financial life:

• If you haven't already done so, share your individual Prosperity Picture with your partner and consider creating a joint Prosperity Picture (as we discussed in Chapter One).

• Review the Financial Wellness Quiz in Chapter Two with your partner and look for areas of connection and disconnection. If there are areas where you see things differently, talk them through.

• Review your net worth statement together. (See the Assets and Liabilities Inventory in Chapter Two.) Make sure each of you not only knows but also understands what you own and what you owe.

• Check in on savings and spending. Are you both satisfied with your current saving and spending levels? (See the section on spending plans in Chapter Two.)

• Review your asset allocation. If you've created an investment portfolio of any kind, including any employer-sponsored plans, such as a 401(k) plan, take a good look at it. What are you each invested in? How has the performance been? Are you both comfortable with the volatility level your investments have shown?

• Are both of you clear, comfortable, and confident with the types and levels of insurance that are in place?

• Review your estate plan. Is it done yet? If not, how can you work together to move it ahead? If it is done, has anything changed that needs to be addressed?

• If you find it challenging to talk with your significant other about money, you may consider making it a threesome . . . and including your financial advisor. For many couples, meetings with their advisor are realistically the only time they cover these financial issues in detail. However you choose to approach it, just make sure you talk about it.

Most important of all, enjoy the process. Money talk doesn't have to be heavy, stressful, or a chore. This is your life together, your money, and your future.

Turning your plan into a reality requires thoughtful action and building the right support for yourself. The internal work of having supportive beliefs and thoughts to aid in your success is crucial to creating a solid foundation. Then setting up systems to save and having the right team there to guide and encourage you will help propel you toward your goals.

Gain Traction Through Action

• Complete the "What Do You Believe About Money?" visualization exercise (see page 119). Reflect on what you uncovered—which of your beliefs are helping you and which are hurting you. Record these in your Prosperity Notebook.

• Use the cancel/clear technique to minimize any negative thoughts around money. Track your progress in your Prosperity Notebook for a week and note any improvements in your frame of mind.

• Create your prosperity priority list. Review and prioritize your goal's list. This will make it easier to work toward your goals without becoming overwhelmed by tackling too many at once or getting distracted by goals that aren't as important to you.

• Clarify what you need to save and invest to meet your goals. Calculate the specific amounts you'll need by using your Prosperity Picture and the Picture Planning questions from Chapter Three as your guide.

• Set up separate flowerpots—separate accounts—to help you save and invest for multiple goals. Arrange for them to be automatically funded from a checking account or your paycheck.

• Establish a solutions cash account. This is a bank account for living expenses funded with enough money to help you sleep at night!

• Plan for what you need to do to accomplish major longer-term goals such as retirement. Take full advantage of any employer-sponsored retirement savings plans available to you or your partner.

• Consider a 529 college savings plan. Learn more at www.sec.gov /investor/pubs/intro529.htm and www.savingforcollege.com.

• Build a strong financial support team. Carefully selected friends, family, and professional advisors can help you clarify your dreams and reach your goals.

• If you don't already work with one, decide whether hiring a financial advisor is right for you. If it seems right, look for someone well suited to help you pursue your personal goals. Check out the Certified Financial Planner site (www.letsmakeaplan.org), the Financial Planning Association (www.plannersearch.org), the

National Association of Personal Financial Advisors (www.napfa
.org) or the National Association of Insurance and Financial Advisors
(www.naifa.org).

• If you're part of a couple, deepen your financial intimacy by making sure you each have a solid understanding of the financial basics
and that you've created a shared vision for your money and life.

Chapter Four Appendix

Key Financial Documents

List the location of applicable items along with any associated online passwords:

- Birth certificate(s)

- Adoption papers

- Marriage license/certificate

- Divorce decree

- Citizenship papers

- Social security cards

- Military service records

- G.I. insurance papers

- Employee benefit plan information

- Insurance policies

  - Life

  - Health care

  - Long term care

  - Disability

  - Auto

  - Homeowner's/renter's

- Umbrella

- Other insurance policy

  - Type

  - Location

- Mortgage/real estate documents

- Auto title(s)

- Property title(s)/deed(s)

- Safe-deposit box

  - Box number

  - Location of key

  - People who have access

- Stock/bond certificates

- Bank accounts

- Investment accounts

- Retirement accounts

- 529 savings plans

- Will(s)/trust documents

- Power of attorney—health care

- Power of attorney—property

- Cemetery plot title(s)

- Tax records

- Business formation documents

- Loan documents

  - Type of loan

  - Location

- Other documents

  - Type

  - Location

- Professional advisors (attorney, financial advisor, accountant, insurance agent, etc.)

    - Name

    - Contact information

Chapter Five

Step Five:
Boost Your Financial Happiness Quotient

The idea of financial "happiness" may seem a bit odd at first because the two concepts aren't typically connected. When's the last time you heard someone say, "Anne is a really financially happy person"? We're more likely to describe our own and others' financial situations in terms of having or not having. "Oh, Laura's a doctor; she's very successful." "Jennifer was born with a silver spoon in her mouth." Or, as Lisa's Italian boss used to say about the owner of a lucrative local auto shop, "He's got the bananas!" On the opposite end of the spectrum, we talk about people who "are low income," "struggle to make ends meet," or "don't have two nickels to rub together." These are all ways of trying to quantify *how much* money a person may have or not have, and often imply some sort of value judgment. But is that really what we want to measure? What if instead of focusing on the amount of money we and others have, we focus on the amount of satisfaction or happiness that money brings us? Know any wealthy people who are miserable, or low-income people who are full of joy? We thought so.

All of us, whether we have little money or lots of money, have the ability to increase our level of financial happiness, and it can be a refreshingly quick and easy thing to do with a huge benefit. If we can increase our financial happiness, we can also increase our ability to experience life with more joy and less stress . . . and again, this works for people of all wealth levels. Let's look at the "more joy" part first.

Giving—even small amounts of money or little gifts—makes almost everyone feel good. Lisa's godson Timmy (the same one who asked for "monies" in exchange for making his bed) recently made a rainbow-colored yarn necklace as a gift for her. He was desperate to give it to her, bursting at the seams for the chance to present it, and elated at her reaction. Even for a boy of seven, it was the act of giving and anticipation of pleasing her that he was so excited about. We know that this isn't unusual and that you can quickly come up with examples like this of your own. We'll explore the science behind giving and how it can be a strategy to increase your financial happiness.

Gratitude works in much the same way. Think of times when someone in your life has expressed true and utter gratitude for something. Think of times when *you* have felt overwhelmingly thankful. Gratitude has a direct link to our financial happiness levels—we'll explore this as well.

And how about the other side of the coin, the "less stress" side? You don't have to reach far here either to come up with examples of life-sucking things people do in the name of money. They stay in unhappy and sometimes abusive marriages so they can maintain a certain lifestyle. They trudge to jobs they hate each day so they can pay the mortgage on houses they may not even like. They spend sleepless nights worrying that their investments might take a turn for the worse or their partners might lose their jobs. We want to change this. Worry is a bad financial planning strategy and financial stress keeps people from using their money as a force for good in their lives. So let's look at ways you can boost not only your prosperity but your financial happiness as well.

Get Out of Debt

Let's tackle stress reduction first. In Chapter Two, we talked about the dangerous trap of credit card debt. You already know that if you're seeking the short-term buzz of buying that perfect accent piece for your living room or that lovely pair of shoes with money you don't have, you'll run up credit card debt. What may not be as obvious is that, once that initial buzz subsides, you may actually end up feeling depressed. Research by Lawrence Berger at the University of Wisconsin–Madison found that a 10 percent increase in credit card debt (as opposed to longer-term debt, like a home mortgage) led to a 14 percent increase in depressive symptoms. Not necessarily clinical depression, but more generalized bummed-out feelings, loss of appetite, and feelings of loneliness.

Sharon is an actor turned attorney who racked up a pile of student loans and $6,000 of credit card debt after she graduated from law school. She paid minimal monthly amounts on both debts, didn't pay much attention to the details, and didn't realize how high her interest rates were. "Then a friend of mine who was in med school and also struggling financially started having debt collectors calling and threatening to turn off his electricity—it was a wake-up call for both of us," she said. Just as Berger's research suggests, Sharon was feeling burdened and depressed as she realized that clothes she was "buying on sale" were taking her years to pay off. She vowed to turn her situation around. She says it was one of the hardest things she's done, and that she spent more than a few nights eating ramen noodles for dinner, but she paid the credit card debt off in one year, paid double on her student loans to get them wiped out in ten years, and has never let herself accrue credit card debt again. Sharon proves it really can be done!

It may seem we're being too black-and-white by saying, "Credit card debt is bad. Saving is good." But, in fact, this is critically important. If you're saddled with credit card debt, the first step toward getting ahead, achieving your goals, and increasing your financial happiness is to get yourself out of debt and stay there. We know it's not easy. Suggesting you reduce your debt by "just making more money and spending less" is like telling someone who wants to lose thirty pounds to exercise more and eat better! It takes vision, inner grit, and know-how, and probably a shift in your belief system to actually follow through on the plan. Luckily, you've already learned some of the key tactics to help you do this:

• The Prosperity Picture you've created for yourself can serve as inspiration for being debt free. Perhaps you have an image of the sailboat trip you'll take to celebrate once you're free of all credit card debt. (Paid for with cash, of course!) This is the equivalent of a dieter hanging a photo of her skinniest self on the refrigerator as inspiration.
• You've already learned some practical suggestions for reducing credit card debt and creating a strategic spending plan from Chapter Two. Think of this as a dieter's meal plan and shopping list.
• And now that you've brushed up on the power of beliefs, you can apply the principles to your beliefs around debt. If they're negative and need shifting, use the ideas from Chapter Four to help yourself. This would be the "Why do you think you *really* ate an entire pizza?" emotional work that dieters often need to face.

As with losing weight, eliminating debt may require as much inner work (or even more) as outer work. Wouldn't it be fabulous to do this at the equivalent of the Biggest Loser Ranch with a trainer constantly reinforcing "You can do this!" to help get you out of debt, shift your habits, and help you experience what it feels like to be a great saver? Just as most people aiming to lose weight won't have this type of support and will need to rely on their own inner voice, you'll likely have to rely on yourself to reduce your debt. Just keep reminding yourself that the payoff is not just better financial health; it's also increased happiness.

Serve Up a Plateful of Grateful

A regular focus on gratitude is another proven way to boost your financial happiness. Gratitude is the no-cost magic elixir to cure many financial (and general life) ills. Focusing on what you are thankful for has been shown to improve overall well-being and happiness. You may have heard before about how turning your attention to what you are grateful for can help you improve your health, experience less stress, sleep better, and maybe even live longer. But did you know that it can actually boost your happiness levels more than doubling your income does?

A practice of focusing on what you are grateful for just five minutes a day can make a big, positive difference in your life. Go ahead right now and write what you're grateful for in your Prosperity Notebook. These can be really big things, such as the health of your family, or smaller things, like the warm cup of tea you're drinking as you are reading. Since this is a book about both your life and your money, you may choose to focus specifically on what you're grateful for financially. Big things: maybe you're thankful for the income you receive from being gainfully employed. But don't forget the small things: perhaps you're grateful that you got a coupon at Starbucks this morning. Take just five minutes to note what you are thankful for today.

Ellen started a gratitude practice with her children when they were very young. Each night as she tucked them into bed they took turns to share five things they were grateful for. When she first began this bedtime ritual, she expected to hear about their toys and electronics. Instead, her son and daughter shared beautiful sentiments such as "I'm grateful for my teachers," "I'm grateful for my friends," and "I'm grateful we are happy, healthy, and safe." One night, when he was ten, her son said: "Mommy, I am so grateful you and Daddy are magnanimous, that we live in such a utopia, and that our life is so fortuitous." Ellen gave Benjy a quizzical look and he replied, "Those are Mrs. Kramer's spelling words this week."

Why did Ellen start this practice with her children? She knew of some of the benefits of gratitude, but she also had a financial education motive in mind. Over the years, Ellen observed that people who were overspenders talked a lot about what they didn't have in their lives. In contrast, the good savers talked about what they were thankful for. Growing the seeds of positive thinking and thankfulness isn't a guarantee of future financial success, but it is worth a try. There is no downside to gratitude, and the upside can be quite big. Here's what some recent research shows:

• Gratitude can reduce materialism. And materialism seems to *reduce* happiness at every income level. So by focusing on gratitude, not only will you help yourself be less materialistic, you'll probably naturally spend less money and be able to save more.

• Grateful people are great to hang out with. Think about the people you most enjoy, the ones you just love spending time with. Chances are they aren't the whiners and complainers. They are likely glass-half-full people who make you feel good about yourself when you're in their presence. We bet they're grateful people who focus on what's working well in their lives. Ellen remembers fondly a woman named Eunice who passed away a few years back. At her funeral, Eunice's daughters and son-in-law commented on how she would always call them after family functions to let them know how much she loved and appreciated the time they spent together. She'd share the specifics of what she enjoyed and how grateful she was to have them in her life. As Ellen heard this, she realized that was one of the reasons she herself enjoyed Eunice so much—Eunice constantly told Ellen what she appreciated about her and how important Ellen was to her. Eunice's gratitude not only was good for Eunice, but it also made Ellen feel like a million bucks.

• This likability factor helps make grateful people better managers, which may help boost their career success. Grateful people have also been found to be more focused and productive—traits that certainly help in career advancement.

• If you are grateful and therefore happier, you may also make more money than your grumpy counterparts. One study revealed that students between ages sixteen and eighteen who described themselves as happier had greater life satisfaction at age twenty-two and earned more by age twenty-nine. Those who described themselves as "very happy teens" ended up earning 10 percent more than the average of people in the study. Gratitude has also been shown to raise optimism levels as well as self-esteem. And people who are highly positive and have strong self-esteem have higher incomes. Again, we can't promise that focusing on gratitude will increase your income, but why not give it a try? You certainly have nothing to lose.

One of the reasons gratitude yields so many benefits is that when you are intentionally focusing on what's working well in your life, you're less likely also to focus on what sucks or what you have no control over. The gratitude pushes out the negative thinking. So when the stock market is going down and your anxiety level is spiking up, take a worry break and focus on what you are grateful for. You can start with being grateful for having money to invest, because many people don't. More than half of all Americans have less than a three-month emergency ("solutions") cushion in savings, and 27 percent have no savings at all. Almost two thirds of people are living paycheck to paycheck. If you happen to be one of them, what can you focus on that's working well? If you have a job, be grateful for that. No job right now? How about your health? Even if everything seems to be crumbling down, can you be grateful for something in this moment? The sun shining or the sounds of the birds? Even in the darkest of times, there's always something to be thankful for.

Here are some ideas for incorporating more gratitude into your daily life:

• Spend five minutes daily writing about what you are grateful for in your Prosperity Notebook. Try to find at least one new thing each day to add to your list.
• If journaling isn't your thing, spend time thinking about what you are thankful for. Ellen reviews her blessings each day when she concludes her meditation. A woman at a workshop in Denver shared with us that whenever she's stopped at a red light, instead of

fiddling with the radio or checking her phone, she uses the time for gratitude thinking. What kind of gratitude practice can you build into your life?

• Feel grateful. As you are writing or thinking about all that rocks in your life, actually *feel* grateful. Ellen's friend Mary calls this "vibrating gratitude."

• Give the gift of gratitude. Each and every day express your gratefulness. Saying thank you and sharing your heartfelt appreciation will not only make you feel good, it but will benefit the recipient as well.

• Write thank-you notes. When we say "write" we mean *actually write*. E-mail notes of appreciation are good, but handwriting a note will surprise and delight the person who receives it.

• Say thank you when you have the opportunity to pay a bill. Most people hate paying their bills. If you still write out your checks by hand, print "Thank you" under your signature in recognition of your gratitude for having the money to pay. If you pay your bills electronically, add your words of thanks in the memo or description section if you have the option. If no option is available, say a word of thanks out loud as you hit the "confirm" button.

• What we appreciate in life appreciates. If you catch yourself complaining, stop. Then find something you can be thankful for instead.

Can Money Make You Happy?

You may have heard that after people reach about $75,000 of income their happiness levels don't increase merely by having more money. This research supports many people's beliefs that what truly makes us happy can't be bought (at least after we have food on the table, a roof over our heads, and health care). But there's a more complex answer to the age-old question of whether money can buy us happiness. Other research suggests that, indeed, having more money *can* make you happier—but it depends on how you use it. It turns out spending on others gives you a bigger happiness boost than spending on yourself. This seems to hold true for people all over the world. So whether you're supporting your local food pantry, sending money to educate kids in another country, or taking a friend out to lunch, it's likely to make you feel happier in the long run than buying this season's "it bag."

This is about shifting from counting your money to counting with your money. Donations to charities, causes, and people who are important to you act as physical manifestations of your gratitude. You don't have to be Bill and Melinda Gates or Oprah Winfrey to make a difference. Merriam-Webster defines "philanthropy" as "the practice of giving money and time to help make life better for other people." We can all do that. The origins of the word "philanthropy" come from the Greek *philanthrōpos*, "loving people." What a beautiful way to build your own prosperity and happiness— through sharing your resources with the vibe of love.

You are likely already a part of the 88 percent of people who donate to causes, institutions, and individuals needing help. Estimates on charitable giving say people give between 2.9 percent and 4.7 percent of their income to charities. Let's explore some of the ways we give to others with our money as well as with our time and energy.

Giving with Your Dollars

• Give with purchase. You've probably experienced the fun of getting a "free gift" with a purchase at some point. Somehow getting a flowered cosmetic bag filled with strange shades of lipstick after you've purchased overpriced makeup seems like you've won a big prize. People will often buy more than they need just to get that freebie. Why not shift your focus from getting gifts with purchases to giving them? Ellen started this with her kids when they were young: with each new toy they brought into the house, they needed to donate an existing one. She now does this herself with clothes. In fact, she jokes that she needs a "sleeveless-dress-buying intervention." When you live in Chicago, you have a short sleeveless dress season, yet she keeps finding ones she thinks are just so cute. So when she brings a new clothing item into her closet, she makes sure to take at least one out to donate. Someone else will benefit and enjoy those things you no longer need or use. Remember to keep your receipt for tax purposes if you donate them to charity.

• Support your friends in their acts of generosity. When your friends ask you to support a cause important to them, say yes! Say yes with your checkbook and wow them with your generosity. Instead of looking at this as an obligation, look at it as a way to support and honor the good work of people in your life.

• Give as you get. Seek out retailers and products that support charities. It might be a percentage of profits or physical items donated to charities. Newman's Own food products, for example, donates all profits from the sales of its products to various worldwide charities. Toms Shoes donates a pair of shoes to a child in need for each pair purchased. Or perhaps you're purchasing fair trade goods that support entrepreneurs around the world through companies such as Ten Thousand Villages or Global Girlfriend. This last one was started by Stacey Edgar to help women around the world gain economic security by providing great products and a way for people to both buy something beautiful and help a woman in need.

• Increase the velocity of your generosity—make giving part of your spending plan. Of course, simply giving cash to causes you care about is one of the most direct ways to spend on others. Most people don't proactively plan the amount of money they'll donate or the individual charities they'll support over the course of a year. Instead, they give when someone asks—sometimes out of inspiration and sometimes out of obligation. But there's a real upside to being more deliberate. Just as saving systematically (through automatic deductions from your checking account) helps boost your savings ability, giving systematically can boost your Financial Happiness Quotient. So consider setting up a "giving account." It can be a simple savings account you use to accumulate money to be given away. Once you set up a giving account, you can turbocharge it by adding to it with a systematic transfer from your checking account. Each week, month, or quarter, authorize a percentage of your income to be moved into your giving account. Why a percentage? This will keep you giving a proportionate amount as your income (hopefully) increases or decreases. It's easy to get thrown off by what initially sounds like a lot of money, so if you use a percentage, you will be less likely to stop your giving when the numbers sound too big. Shortly after Ellen and her husband started their giving account, one of their pet charities asked for a specific large donation. Ellen's first reaction was "Wow, that's so much money!" She then realized they had three times that amount already sitting in their giving account!

Another benefit of automatically funding your giving account is that it can support you in giving even when things feel tight.

During the depths of the recession people tightened up significantly on their giving at the precise time charities saw their greatest need. When you stop giving because you are scared, you are putting a kink in the hose of prosperity flowing to you. We're certainly not saying you should give more than you can afford, but we are suggesting that when you focus on others who are less fortunate, especially during tough times, you potentially create a positive and powerful loop. Here's how it works:

- Your thoughts are focused on others' problems and how you can help them (the "how you can help them" part is directly connected to your blessings).
- Because your thoughts are focused on your blessings, it's impossible for your thoughts to be focused on your problems (your challenges).
- Where thoughts go, energy flows.
- This process brings more energy to your blessings—and helps you feel better along the way.

Our dear friend Melissa recently experienced a variation of this phenomenon when she was having a particularly bad day. She had just left her doctor's office after having had a miscarriage and was feeling very down. It was a perilously cold day and as she was sitting in her car at a traffic light a homeless man with a sign asking for money approached her car. It was so cold that he had tears in his eyes, and when Melissa saw the look on his face, she reached into her bag and pulled out the cash she had—a twenty-dollar bill—and gave it to him. He was very, very grateful for her gift, and she recalls clearly that, at that moment, her own pain lessened significantly. By giving him the money, she was focusing on her blessings, not on her challenges. It's a powerful concept. Give it a try and see what happens for you!

Let the Government Help You Give

Your charitable giving may also give you a tax benefit. It's like a gift with purchase from the government. You give to a qualified charity and the federal government lets you deduct part or all of your contribution on your federal income taxes. Here are some things to keep in mind:

• Your contribution must be made to a qualified charitable organization. So your nephew who needs some extra support is not a tax-deductible contribution. Neither are contributions to political organizations or candidates. Check IRS Publication 526 on the IRS.gov Web site for more information on qualified charitable organizations (www.irs.gov/uac/Publication-526,-Charitable-Contributions-1).

• To deduct the contribution, you must file a tax return and itemize your deductions.

• If you get something in return for your contribution (like that spa package you won at the silent auction or the airline ticket you won in a raffle), you can deduct only the amount you contributed that exceeds the value of what you received. So if you spent $200 on a massage that was valued at $150, you can deduct $50 on your tax return.

• If you donate stock or other noncash items, your deduction is usually for the fair market value of your donation. So if you donate the car you bought for $15,000 ten years ago, you can deduct only the $3,000 it is now worth on your tax return.

• If you donate clothes or household items, they need to be in good usable condition to be eligible for deduction. IRS Publication 561 can help you determine the value (www.irs.gov/pub/irs-pdf/p561.pdf).

• Remember to keep good records. If you contribute more than $250, you must have bank records, payroll deduction records, or an acknowledgment from the qualified charity to be able to deduct the contribution. If you make noncash contributions (for stuff you gave away) in excess of $500, you have to complete a separate tax form. Ellen and her husband were audited for their charitable contributions and were able to provide backup for each contribution made. This helped them get through the audit process quickly, and relatively painlessly.

If you give larger amounts of money ($1,000 or more) to certain charities, consider donating stocks or mutual funds that have grown in value. If you give stock to a charity, they have the ability to sell it without paying capital gains taxes. This will potentially save you money, because if you were to sell the stock, you would have to pay tax on your gain. Also, if you are giving large amounts of money, consider getting professional advice from an attorney, tax advisor, or financial advisor to help you make sure you are getting all the tax benefits you deserve. There are many tax-saving strategies that can be used not only to help the charity, but to help you and your family as well.

Giving of Your Time and Energy

There are lots of ways beyond money to give, all of which can have a halo effect over your financial happiness. One well-researched type of giving is "generativity." Stephen Post and Jill Neimark explain the concept in *Why Good Things Happen to Good People* as nurturing others to manifest *their* strengths and gifts—a way of "helping another prepare their garden for spring." It can be as simple as listening, caring, and helping others to renew their sense of self and hope.

Generativity can be powerful. Teens who are generative in high school live significantly longer, healthier, and happier lives than their less giving peers. Being a nurturing person when you are young continues into adulthood and provides the added benefit of protecting your physical and mental health. It's also linked to success and self-esteem in adulthood. Generativity in older adults helps protect and improve psychological well-being and extends life span.

Think about your own experiences with giving and how you felt afterward. We are led to give because it feels great to do so. There is a wonderful feedback loop—giving to others bounces back and feels great for us. Take out your Prosperity Notebook and jot down examples of times you gave to others and how you felt after your act of service. And we're not necessarily talking about major acts like donating a kidney (although if you have, we say well done!)—small acts of generosity themselves are often of immeasurable value.

Ellen remembers returning to her car in a parking garage when she ran into a woman on the elevator who smiled at her and said, "I can't seem to remember where I parked my car." Ellen smiled back and wished her luck. As she was driving out a few minutes later, Ellen saw the woman wandering the aisles. She stopped and told her, "Get in—we'll look for your car together." They drove around for almost fifteen minutes, and just as Ellen was about to give up and drop the woman off at the garage office, she spotted her car. She looked at Ellen and said, "Thank you so much—I'm a nun and

I'll pray for you!" The woman got to find her car, but Ellen got rewarded as well: she felt a true jolt of happiness from being of service, not to mention the added bonus of a prayer. (Even as a Jew she knew it must be pretty good to have a nun pray for you!) She still feels good when she remembers this story. This very small act created a big boost in her happiness that has lasted a long time.

What if you were able to combine some of your Prosperity Picture goals with a giving component? For example, Ellen has the airplane image on her Picture, which to her represents travel; this is one of her major passions in life. She also has an image of her family to reflect how important it is to her to stay close and connected with her husband and kids. In addition, she has the volunteer image to remind her of the goal to give on a regular basis. As a busy working mom, Ellen found a way to combine all three of these goals in a fabulous way. When her kids were eleven and thirteen, they started taking volunteer vacations as a family. Their first trip was to Costa Rica to help a local group serve elderly and disabled people in the community. They've since been to Ghana several times to work in the schools and help with construction and to Peru to work in an orphanage.

These trips were amazing experiences for the entire family on many levels. First, the kids were able to meet and play with other kids from totally different parts of the world and realize they weren't really that different. They learned that although the kids they met had very little in terms of material possessions, they were rich in happiness. Even at young ages, Amy and Benjy learned they had something to give and share. In Ghana, they ended up teaching a class of fourth-graders for four days because their teacher was absent (no substitute teachers at this school). Twelve-year-old Amy and fourteen-year-old Benjy became known as Madam Amy and Sir Benjy to their new students! These novice teachers kept the students engaged by playing math and word games as well as enjoying plenty of recess time. By contrast, Ellen, her husband Steven, and his sister Gail lost total control over their classrooms when they attempted to teach a lesson even for a couple of hours! The whole family was also able to see new places, taste new foods, and experience all the benefits travel has to offer.

How might you incorporate more giving and acts of service into your life?

• Review your Prosperity Picture. Do any of your images and the corresponding goals have a generative quality? Note in your Prosperity Notebook how your goals will support others in their growth. For example, do any of the goals have elements of mentoring others, volunteering, or raising happy, healthy kids? If not, consider adding some images or thinking more deeply about the meaning of images you've already chosen.

• Volunteer for an organization, cause, or campaign that feeds your soul. You'll not only make a difference for others and meet new people, but you just might increase your longevity! If you're not sure where you want to give your time, try out different options. Your employer may allow service days, your community may offer volunteer opportunities, or there may be organizations that offer a variety of short-term ways to contribute your time and talent.

• Be a kind-act-doer. Look for small ways to make a positive difference in the lives of others. Maybe you have a friend who needs a shoulder to cry on or a caring person just to listen. Something as easy as a smile can make a positive difference to even a passing stranger. Each day make sure to perform at least one kind act. Note these in your Prosperity Notebook.

Giving to Grow Your Affluence and Your Influence

You've probably already experienced some of the juiciness associated with giving to others. But did you know that giving can also make you rich? A big claim, we know, but PhD, author, and conservative think tank president Arthur Brooks found in his research that people who give to charity make significantly more money. Our first reaction is, "Well, of course they do—that's how they can afford to give." And it's true that charitable contributions do increase as people's income goes up. But get this—as people give more, their incomes actually *increase.* Let us say that again. Brooks found that as people's charitable contributions increased, they actually made more money. Imagine two similar families who have the same income, number of kids, and level of education. The difference between the two is that one family donates $100 more this year to charity than the other family. Brooks found in his analysis that the family who donated the extra money will earn an average of $375 more income that year than the other one!

He observed this phenomenon working not just with individuals but also within entire countries. As individual charitable contributions increase, so does the gross domestic product (GDP) of the country where those individuals live. His analysis showed that every $100 contribution increased GDP by an average of $1,800. So your giving will, at a minimum, help the charity you give it to, but also has the potential to boost your income and the entire economy! Not a bad outcome.

All of this may sound odd at first. How can this possibly be? Is this rise in wealth explained by the metaphysical concept that what goes around comes around? Although we do strongly believe that what you put out in the world comes back to you, research has found something more tangible as well. It turns out that giving money away and spending your resources on others increases your feeling of wealth—researchers call this "subjective wealth." When you give money away, there's a feeling you must be doing well enough to be able to do so. You feel happier as a result. And, as we've just pointed out, happier people are demonstrably more successful in their careers . . . and earn more money. Think of it as a simple equation: Giving is likely to make you feel happy. When you feel happy, your self-esteem is likely to increase. When your self-esteem increases, your performance is likely to improve. When your performance improves, you're likely to do better at work. When you do better at work, you're likely to earn more money. Does this formula work every time? Nope. Does it work a lot of the time? Absolutely. The research bears it out. (By the way, if you're very skeptical about the possibility of this phenomenon, might it be *less* likely to happen for you personally? Probably so. So consider what might happen for you if you open yourself up to the possibilities here.)

And there's more! Michael Norton, a Harvard Business School professor and coauthor of *Happy Money: The Science of Smarter Spending*, found that giving away $500 had the same effect on subjective wealth feelings as earning an extra $10,000. How cool is that? Norton also found that when people feel wealthier from the act of donating money, it diminishes the need for conspicuous consumption. So donating to charity may also contribute to our bottom lines by helping us trim spending.

How Can I Give if I Feel I Don't Have Enough?

Still not convinced that donating money will make you feel wealthier and ultimately increase your income? Are you wondering, "How can I give if I am worried about not having enough?" That feeling is the exact reason *to* give. If you are hanging on so tightly to what you have, you'll be unable to receive what is coming your way.

Think of giving and receiving as being mutually supporting in the same way that inhaling and exhaling are. If we only inhaled air—received it—we would die. Likewise, if all we did was exhale—give—air, the outcome would, ultimately, be the same.

So giving and receiving of our resources, time, and energy is interrelated in much the same way. Believing there is enough—having the feeling of plenty—can lead you to give, grow, and even tangibly prosper. One year, during the holidays, Lisa made a decision to give money to anyone who asked. This included friends asking for donations to their favorite charities, organizations that Lisa and her family support, and people on the street asking for money. She didn't designate a specific dollar amount, just that she would give something to anyone who asked. Within two weeks of her decision, she got a letter in the mail from one of her credit cards explaining that there had been a class-action lawsuit settlement related to the credit-monitoring service fees she had been paying for years and cardholders were entitled to a full refund of their fees. She looked closer and saw that she had a $500 credit on her statement! She had made a specific decision to "loosen her grip" on money that holiday season. Was that why she got the $500 credit? Depends on what you believe. Objectively, of course, one has nothing to do with the other. But if we look at things from a different perspective, could there be a deeper relationship between the two events? We think so. Try opening your mind to the possibility and give it a shot yourself. See what happens!

It's *Not* Better to Give Than to Receive

For some people, giving is the easy part. They grow up hearing it's better to give than to receive. They know how good it feels to help others and are happy to do so. But when it comes to receiving, well, that's just not their thing. Know anyone like that . . . maybe very personally? Well, we have an insight to share that may be a bit startling: it's *not* better to give than to receive. They are *both* important. There needs to be someone on the other side of the giving to receive. Sometimes we need to give and sometimes we need to receive. People who are always giving—whether of their time, expertise, or money—will eventually either burn out or run out of precious resources. By the same token, people who are always taking, mooching, or demanding more than their fair share will probably never experience true prosperity. They may end up with material wealth (if they don't land themselves in jail), but they may also end up alienating people around them and feeling lonely, isolated, and unhappy. Balance is crucial.

Here's another way to look at it. We've talked about the good feelings generated through acts of service. Well, if you don't let others give to you, you are diminishing their ability to feel good. Interesting perspective, huh? We see this show up in both big and small ways. Have you ever received a compliment and either deflected it or threw a compliment right back at the person? It might sound something like this:

Melanie: "Wow, Betsy, you really look great in that outfit!"

Betsy: "Oh, this . . . I've had this for ages."

Couldn't Betsy have just said thank you?

It could even be what you say to yourself that closes you off to receiving. Ellen remembers a conversation she had while getting her makeup professionally done. The makeup artist said, "Your skin is really nice." Not believing she had good skin, Ellen immediately thought, "I bet she tells that to everyone." When you don't accept a compliment graciously, you are, in a small way, pushing away abundance and not honoring the person who gave it to you.

This phenomenon can show up in other, more concrete ways as well. Lisa's grandmother Angelina was a generous woman who passed away at age ninety-four. In her lifetime she gave her family and friends many beautiful gifts, and never let even minor holidays like Valentine's Day pass without giving her grandchildren money. It was very important for her to give. In fact, at one point Lisa's mom tried to intervene by pointing out that it wasn't necessary to give money to the grandkids for every single holiday. Angelina wouldn't hear of it. Never one to have a problem with candor, she looked at Lisa's mom and said, "Of *course* I'm going to give them money! When I die, I don't want them to look back on me and think, 'Well, she was a cheap son of a bitch.'" A big giver and also a true character!

But here's the thing—Angelina also had a really hard time receiving. For most of her life, the moment she saw any member of the family approach her with a wrapped present for any special occasion, she would immediately become agitated. "Jo, what did you go and do now? You shouldn't be spending money on me! Are you crazy? Take it back to the store!" And all before she even took the bow off! We know she was grateful for gifts, but sometimes she couldn't even say thank you out loud—not because she wasn't appreciative, but because it really did make her feel bad that her family and friends were spending money on her.

Lisa, a proverbial apple that didn't fall far from the tree, has to be vigilant that she doesn't fall into the same trap. Once on her birthday she invited some friends over to celebrate with cocktails, and many of those friends brought her lovely and unexpected gifts. She was touched and appreciative, but also had a strong dose of the same kind of resistance her grandmother used to have. She felt bad they had spent money on her and embarrassed that they might have thought she expected a gift. That evening she rode it out and focused on being grateful for her lovely friends and their generosity rather than being self-conscious about receiving—but it's something she needs to pay attention to.

These might seem like trivial examples, but they reflect the many ways people block abundance flowing to them. Did you know that 70 percent of people receiving windfalls will lose most of it within several years? If you aren't open to receiving and ready to be a good steward of your money, it could slip through your hands like sand.

Remember playing on a teeter-totter as a kid? If you had a friend on the other side who was about your size, it was easy to go up and down. Maybe you even tried to balance with both of you off the ground. If your friend was much bigger than you, it was fun at first because as they went down you went up really fast, but after a while it wasn't fun for them because you couldn't give them as exciting a ride. Giving and receiving is kind of like a teeter-totter. Sometimes it's your turn to go up and sometimes it's your turn to go down. The joy is sucked out pretty quickly if you're always the one up in the air or always the one down on the ground. Your next step may be to increase your contributions to others or maybe to be more receptive. We encourage you to be awake and aware of the cycle of giving and receiving happening all the time.

We've covered all sorts of ways to increase your financial happiness, many of which involve focusing outside of yourself and doing so with gratitude. When you take the spotlight off yourself and shine a light on the world around you, the results are amazing. In short order you'll find you feel calm, confident, and connected. These feelings will not only lead to lower stress, but may also allow you to make better, more rewarding financial decisions.

Gain Traction Through Action

• Reduce your debt. If you have credit card debt, commit to yourself that you'll find a way to reduce or eliminate it. The relief you'll feel is likely to be enormous and will provide a huge boost to your Financial Happiness Quotient.

• Create a daily gratitude practice. Set aside five minutes a day to focus on what you're grateful for—big things and small. Write these down in your Prosperity Notebook, say them out loud, or review them meditatively. Notice the effect it begins to have on your happiness and well-being.

• Decide to make a difference. Spend time considering how you currently give to others. What can you do to give even more effectively?

• Set up a giving account. Have a percentage of your income transferred to this account on a regular basis. Deliberately plan how you will give away this money to support causes and people important to you.

• Shift your perspective from problems to possibilities. The next time you're feeling low, try giving as antidote—focusing on your blessings instead of your challenges may make all the difference!

• Let the government help you give. Take advantage of tax benefits associated with your charitable contributions. Questions? For more information go to www.irs.gov/uac/Publication-526,-Charitable-Contributions-1.

• Give with purchase. When you buy something new, make sure to give something away. You might even get a tax deduction for this. For more information, go to www.irs.gov/pub/irs-pdf/p561.pdf.

• Amp up your "generativity." Use your Prosperity Picture as inspiration to think about ways you might support others and boost acts of kindness beyond what you already do. You'll not only help others but also help yourself in the process.

• Be a great giver and a great receiver. Check in with yourself on your openness to both giving and receiving. Remember that swinging too far one way or the other can block your prosperity.

Chapter Six

Step Six:
Become Financially Resilient

Remember the story of the three little pigs? One pig built a house of straw, one of wood, and one of bricks. They all faced the same threat: the big bad wolf. But only the pig that built the house of bricks was able to stay protected and safe.

How can you build your financial house to withstand the big bad economy? How can you create a sound foundation to be able to handle whatever comes your way and still create your Prosperity Picture? It takes both internal resilience, so you can continue to make sound decisions, and external resilience, to build a sound financial structure.

Let's start from the foundation and work our way up.

Building on Solid Ground

One of the most effective ways to stay financially centered is to spend as much time as possible in what we call the "Prosperity Zone." Sadly, most people don't do this. Instead, they live most of their lives in the opposite place: a frightened, worried state of mind we call "Scare-City."

Just about everyone has felt occasional fear or concern about some aspect of their finances—that's part of life. But here's the problem: when you spend a majority of your time and attention on the difficulties of your financial situation, the money problems of people in your circles, and "this terrible economy" in general, your ability to create true wealth can actually be impaired. Seeing the world through dark-colored glasses can get you stuck in Scare-City with no clear path out.

How do you know if you're hanging out there? Well, it might show up as seeing limited opportunities in front of you. Have you ever said, "I'll never have a chance to travel where I want," "I'm too old to find a job," or "There are no good men out there"? (This negative thinking doesn't just happen with money.) Those may be Scare-City clues. It can also look like what Ellen's mom used to call "sour grapes"—feeling negative when something good happens to someone you know. For example, let's say your friend gets a new job that she's super excited about. You smile and congratulate her, but deep inside you're actually thinking it's not fair, she always gets everything she wants without even trying, and she looks fat in her pants. Why? Quite possibly because being stuck in Scare-City can bring out that kind of "You win; I lose" thinking and aggressive competition, and can lead to feelings of envy and resentment. This is especially true if you happen to feel stuck in a situation you're not happy with. Being in Scare-City can also lead you to blame others for things you're unhappy with in your own life instead of taking responsibility for them yourself. And retelling yourself over and over the story of how you were wronged is a perfect way to take up permanent residence there!

Let's take a look at Leslie, who unfortunately has spent a lot of time in Scare-City. Leslie was in a very unhappy marriage. She knew her husband Bill was a gambler and overspender and also suspected he was being secretive about some of his money dealings. Still, Leslie didn't consider herself a "financial person," so she didn't ask Bill many questions and more or less turned the financial reins almost completely over to him. She was unhappy enough to contemplate divorce, and even went so far as to see an attorney, but before she got up the nerve to tell Bill she wanted out he became gravely ill and died. As she sorted through the pieces after his death, Leslie discovered that, unbeknown to her, her husband had spent most of an inheritance she had received from her grandmother and had also run up tens of thousands of dollars in credit card debt, leaving her in a very difficult situation.

Now, was Leslie's husband irresponsible? You bet. And we don't mean to sound unsympathetic here, but so was she. She didn't trust her feelings that her husband wasn't acting in their best interest and she let herself be guided by her false belief that she wasn't capable of handling financial decisions herself. Years later, she's still blaming her late husband for her financial situation. She's stuck in her story and doesn't have a lot of energy left to improve or even objectively see her finances. It may be easier to point the finger at someone else, and sometimes it can initially feel gratifying to make someone else wrong, but by doing so we push ourselves closer and closer toward victimhood. And victims, by definition, don't have much power. True prosperity begins when we can step into full accountability for our own situations. When bad things happen, there is incredible opportunity for growth and learning if you're willing to see your part in the situation.

So, How Do We Move Out of Scare-City and into the Prosperity Zone?

Have you ever known someone who, no matter what's happening in the economy or in their personal life, is able to prosper? Hannah is one of those people. She's a graphic designer who really stands out from the crowd. While many of her peers struggle to make a living, she earns about eight times the national average. She works for herself and sets her own hours. Even during recessionary times, Hannah's income has been stable. Amazingly, she has also been able to keep this abundance flowing in other aspects of her life, even when times are tough. Several years ago Hannah got the sad news that her brother was diagnosed with prostate cancer, and she knew she wanted to help in every way possible. Lots of people would be derailed by this and would focus almost solely on the tragedy in their lives. Not Hannah. She was able to rally support, spend a great deal of time with her brother before his eventual death, and still somehow keep her business going strong.

What's Hannah's secret? How does she stay in the Prosperity Zone? Hannah intuitively knows the keys to keep abundance flowing, even in the face of challenging situations. We'll share what she does and what you can do too.

Shift Your Perspective

The first thing to do is to take a step back and think about how you're approaching a given situation. We just love this quote from transformational author Byron Katie:

"Life is simple. Everything happens for you, not to you.

Everything happens at exactly the right moment, neither too soon nor too late. You don't have to like it . . . it's just easier if you do."

Much of our stress and pain (well, maybe even all of it) comes from how we view the situations we find ourselves in. If you can see events as happening *for* you, not *to* you, it's so much easier to both find the lesson or gift in a situation and also see possible ways out. We know this is often easier said than done—in the midst of a terrible situation it's not always easy to find the blessings.

Interestingly, kids often do a great job of teaching us how to do this. On a trip to Fort Myers, Florida, to speak for a charitable foundation, Ellen experienced plane-shaking turbulence. Not the kind where you feel a few bumps. The kind where the coffee flies out of your cup, your stomach lurches up in your body, and you wonder why you said no to that chocolate chip bread pudding at dinner if it was just going to end like this. Lots of passengers were screaming and clutching their armrests, and everyone seemed terrified. Out of the corner of her eye, Ellen noticed two kids sitting across the aisle from her. As she looked over at these grade-school-age children traveling with their mom, she saw that not only were they not screaming, they actually had huge smiles on their faces. As she caught their eye, they laughed and said, "That was so much fun! Can we do it again?" It's all about how you look at things!

Is stock market volatility horrible? Or could it be an opportunity to buy at a good price? Is losing your job terrible? Or is it a chance to try something new and potentially more fulfilling or lucrative? Is it possible that financial turmoil could be a path to being a better person, becoming stronger, and growing wiser? We say absolutely—but only if you are ready and willing to see it that way. Having this viewpoint is critical for building resilience from the core and being in the Prosperity Zone.

Find the Upside in a Down Situation

The next way to keep abundance flowing during a period of difficulty is to look for specific ways you can use a given challenge to improve your life. Financial ups and downs can be opportunities for amazing personal growth. If everything happens to teach us something useful, then the question to ask is not *if* a crummy situation is meant to be a lesson or learning opportunity, but *what* that opportunity is. We must ask, "What is the benefit and good that could arise from this circumstance?"

Brenda lost her advertising job during a financial downturn. It took her nineteen months to find another job, but fortunately she had been a good saver who lived below her income level, and by cutting back on expenses was able to live on her unemployment checks and a small amount of her savings. Working with her financial advisor, she determined that, though she didn't want to, if she *had* to she could afford to retire right then as long as she kept her expenses very low. Though this provided her some relief, she was nonetheless filled with anxiety about not having a steady income again.

She eventually got a job offer at a lower salary, for work she wasn't excited about and didn't really want. But at the time she was living right in the middle of downtown Scare-City and, motivated by fear, she took the job just so she could get a regular paycheck. Six months later and seemingly out of the blue, she was diagnosed with cancer. As Brenda faced this very difficult life event, she examined her situation and her options and realized there was really no reason to stay in a job she hated. So she left the job and attended to her health.

Shortly after she made this freeing decision, and much to her surprise and delight, she was offered a job at a firm she loved! Thankfully, she also came through her health issues strong and well. In this process she clearly saw that making fear-based decisions, even though at the time she thought those decisions would ease her stress, is a mistake. Brenda found the upside in a very down situation, and her challenges with money led her to discover what was really important in her life. It led her into the Prosperity Zone.

Be Financially Creative

Challenging times can also be an opportunity to amp up your creativity. This will help open the flow of money back into your life. Instead of viewing a difficult financial period as a crushing defeat, see it as an opportunity for something new to emerge.

Years ago Ellen and her husband Steven visited Mount Saint Helens in Washington, where she saw a great analogy for such new growth out of difficulty. You might remember that on May 18, 1980, the most deadly and costly volcanic eruption in U.S. history occurred there. The effects on the environment were massive—in the 143-square-mile blow zone closest to the volcano, trees toppled and the ground was covered with layers of ash; in many areas no remnants of the former forest remained at all. It was depressing, desolate, and seemed forever ruined. However, within a relatively short amount of time, something amazing happened: little shoots of green began to emerge, animals started appearing again, insects started flying around! It didn't seem possible, but there it was. These new signs of life continued and grew stronger and more robust over time. Today, though the area isn't exactly the same as it was before the eruption, and never will be, it's beautiful again in a whole new way.

Your financial life can also come back after a crisis. It probably won't look the same as it did before the jolt to your financial ecosystem, but different isn't necessarily a bad thing. Tara and her husband Andy owned a restaurant in Dallas for nine years, and it was doing so well that they decided to get a bank loan to open a second location. The food critics loved the restaurants and so did their customers—they were crazy busy all the time. Unfortunately, the economy started to slow, and their business began to slow too. To make matters worse, the city decided to replace the sewer pipes and dug up the road and sidewalk right in front of their second location.

One day, the banker in charge of Tara and Andy's loan casually asked how things were going. She said, "Well, business is down, but picking up a little bit." She went on to say that as soon as the construction was completed she was sure they'd see a big spike in customers, that they had a seven-month reserve of cash to help them through this slow time, and that their investors were supportive of their plans. The following Monday Tara got a call from one of her waiters saying that his paycheck had bounced, and when he called to ask why, the bank informed him there were no funds in the company account to cover his check. Without notice to Tara or Andy, the bank had called back their loan and frozen their accounts! Unable to find another bank to help and with no access to funds, they were forced to close both restaurants. Without the income from their businesses, Tara and Andy had no money to pay their bills. They ended up declaring bankruptcy and losing their home to foreclosure.

Are you wondering how there can be anything good that comes

out of this story? Believe it or not, there is. And it begins with the fact that, despite their difficulties, Tara and Andy were open to looking at their life in a new way. They saw they had two choices: stay stuck in fear and anger and blame the economy and the bankers—*or* find the message in this mess. They chose the latter.

Tara and Andy realized that, though they were good at it, they never really loved being in the food business. Although they had talked about doing something different, their early success swayed them to continue. Uncertain of the next move, and with lots of free time on his hands, Andy took Tara's old art supplies out of the basement and started painting. He was quite talented and found he loved the process. Today he is following his passion and has found a way to monetize it by selling his artwork. Tara started talking with friends, meeting new people, and eventually carved out a niche for herself doing computer graphics for women-owned businesses across the country. She loves her clients and loves that she can set her own hours. Without being tied to their businesses, they also realized they were no longer tied to Dallas. Tara and Andy had always loved Colorado, so they picked up and moved there. They now have more time to be with their children and have decided to home-school them. None of this would have happened if their restaurants hadn't failed. When asked about this, Tara said, "I knew we needed to make changes in our life—I would have much rather made the changes proactively, but given the success we were having, that wouldn't have happened. Yes, it was hard, but having the bank call our loans was ultimately one of the best things that could have happened to us. We are now so happy, doing work we love and able to spend wonderful time with our kids." Different, sure, but certainly not bad.

When faced with a challenging financial situation, grab your

Prosperity Notebook and write down your answers to these questions:

- If there was a really good reason this was happening, what could it be?
- Am I open to the possibility that this is happening *for* me and not *to* me?
- How can I be creative in the face of this adversity?
- When I get through this, what skills will I have developed? (For example, learning how to be more frugal, more assertive, calmer in the face of pressure, or more focused on the most important things.)
- In one year will I still be upset by this?
- If it were five years from now and I was telling a friend about this situation, I would tell them I learned . . .

Create Financial Tranquillity

Another way to stay in the Prosperity Zone and away from Scare-City is to build your self-calming skills. Having the ability to soothe yourself during turbulent financial times is crucial for effective money management. When the world looks different from our expectations, it's easy to feel stressed out and scared. At precisely the time creativity and a clear head are indispensable, these nervous feelings can limit our ability to find optimal solutions. That's why you need to use techniques to still your mind, help you feel calm, and improve your ability to accept the present circumstances. From this place of calm, you can move forward and implement new strategies.

Not so keen on implementing a new strategy when the world seems like it's falling apart around you? We get that. We've read plenty of articles that suggest you do something like "go jogging" to get over a bad breakup. Even though we all know that physical exercise, fresh air, and mental distraction really might be helpful in such a situation, it may seem, in the moment, like a ridiculous suggestion. Go *jogging* to combat heartbreak? What about a pint of good old Ben & Jerry's and a family-sized jug of Merlot? Look at it this way: if you're worried or upset about something and find yourself continually wallowing in those negative emotions, resisting reality, and wishing your circumstances were different, you are actually *keeping* yourself stuck and increasing your suffering. Don't get us wrong—learning to be comfortable exactly where you are right now doesn't mean you're giving up. It just means you aren't fighting the reality of the situation. With this acceptance, you will very likely surprise yourself by finding renewed direction and energy.

So how can you relax the grip of worry? Here's one of our favorite strategies:

Breathe Your Financial Stress Away

Sounds too simplistic? Humor us and try it. Take in a full deep breath. Breathe in through your nose to the count of four: one, two, three, four. Now exhale to the count of six: one, two, three, four, five, six. Try it again. Inhale: one, two, three, four. Exhale: one, two, three, four, five, six. One more time. Inhale: one, two, three, four. Exhale: one, two, three, four, five, six. How do you feel? A little more relaxed?

Here's a quick peek at what's going on inside your body. When people experience stress, the body is hardwired to increase the heartbeat and divert blood away from your core to your limbs. This is a survival instinct because those shifts can help us physically run away. If a woolly mammoth is chasing you, this is a perfect response and could help you save your own life. If your 401(k) plan drops by 30 percent, not so much! Breathing is a way to neutralize that stress reaction. Scientific research shows that deep breathing reduces the stress hormones in your body. Through deep breathing, your respiratory system sends messages to your brain that quickly calm the centers involved in thought, emotion, and behavior.

Breathing is unique because it happens without our having to think about it and yet we always have the option to deliberately focus on our breath and change its depth and rhythm. Learning to do this, and thereby manage our natural stress reactions, is important for physical health. Too much stress for too long increases the release of the hormone cortisol, which in turn can reduce your immune system's ability to fight off infection.

Stress also changes how you make decisions. Research reveals that when people are under stress they tend to focus on positive factors and ignore negative ones as they make decisions. For example, stressed-out people considering a new job might let themselves be more influenced by a higher salary than by a horrific commute. Stress-induced focus on the upside may also play a role in addictions. Ever been a little freaked out and go for just one . . . or three . . . or ten more of those frozen Thin Mint Girl Scout cookies? Exactly.

Researchers also found that stress increases the differences in the ways men and women look at risk. When stress rises for men, they tend to increase their risk, whereas when stress rises for women, they get more conservative about risk.

So merely focusing on your breathing, and therefore reducing your stress, can actually help you to become healthier, wealthier, and savvier.

Say Om to Get Mo'

Really want to calm down about money? Take it to the next level by establishing a regular practice to quiet your mind. Many find yoga and meditation fabulous ways to bring more peace to every area of life. Money, yoga, meditation . . . really? Harking back to *Sesame Street* days, you might be hearing that song in your head: "One of these things is not like the others. One of these things doesn't belong." It may seem strange at first, but yoga and meditation really can be pathways to financial success.

Let's go back to Scare-City and look at it more closely. Researchers Sendhil Mullainathan and Eldar Shafir define scarcity as having less than you feel you need. What they found is that "scarcity directly reduces bandwidth—not a person's inherent capacity, but how much of that capacity is currently available for use." Their research found that merely mentioning money challenges to people living below the poverty level hurt their cognitive performance even more than extreme sleep deprivation. This group's IQ scores could actually temporarily drop by as much as 13 points when faced with scarcity concerns. Of course, being financially stressed doesn't mean someone isn't smart, but it can mean their ability to make good decisions at that point is greatly compromised. Conclusion? Financial worries can deprive you of the mental capacity to find your way out of your financial difficulties.

Here's where meditation comes in—it's a great way to

neutralize that stress. But, you may ask, can meditation really help with financial worries? You bet it can! Not only does a regular practice of meditation help you to feel more relaxed and neutralize your stress, but some types of meditation practices have been found to actually *increase* creative thinking and problem-solving abilities.

Have you ever had so many programs open on your computer that it freezes? This used to happen to Ellen all the time. Scott, her computer guy, told her she was a "superuser." That made her feel like a big deal for a second, but then she realized all it meant was that her computer wouldn't operate efficiently until she did something about it. The short-term fix was to continually reboot the computer. This wasted time and drove her nuts. The better fix was either to stop trying to do so many things at once or to get a more powerful processor.

Do you ever feel like a superuser of your own brain? As if you have too many thoughts, tasks, and concerns buzzing at the same time? Meditation is akin to getting a more powerful processor. Our minds can get so cluttered with constant chatter that we can't hear the wisdom inside of us. Meditation helps to quiet the static noise so you can better tune in to hear insights and see opportunities.

It can feel quite normal to have a constant stream of thoughts floating through our minds—so normal that we don't even realize we aren't performing optimally. But after you have an opportunity to calm and quiet your mind—especially if you can develop a habit and do it on a regular basis—you'll notice more mental clarity and more quiet moments between thoughts.

If you don't meditate already, you might not even understand what you're missing until you start doing it. Ellen was driving through a nearby suburb and saw a man in a parking lot with what looked like an old bicycle attached to a round sharpening stone. It turned out he was sharpening knives. Intrigued by this, she imme-diately drove home to get her knife set that hadn't been sharpened since she'd received it as a wedding gift eighteen years earlier. The man sharpened them and told Ellen she had a very nice set of knives but needed to take better care of them. She couldn't believe how well they worked once they were sharpened. She had gotten so used to working with dull knives that she had begun to think she hated making dishes that required a lot of chopping. Once her knives were in good working condition, Ellen found cooking prep much easier and more enjoyable. A regular practice of meditation is like sharpening your mental knives. You'll feel more clarity, be more focused, and have more energy to easily handle financial and other challenges that come your way.

There are many different ways to meditate. If you are new to meditation, here are some suggestions to get you started. First, de-cide how long you want to meditate—even just five minutes is a fine amount to start. You can work your way up to longer time periods and even multiple times per day if you desire. Next, find a quiet location where you'll be undisturbed. Remember to turn off your phone—anyone trying to reach you can wait until you're done meditating. Are you worrying about needing to get your body into seated pretzel position? Let that one go—any comfortable seated position is just fine. You probably don't want to lie down or you might find yourself snoring through your meditation.

Okay, you're in a quiet, comfortable place—now what? One easy way to start is to focus your attention on your breathing. No-tice the air coming in, filling your body; then slowly exhale. Breathe in and breathe out. Just watch your breathing. When thoughts come up, and they will, don't worry. Our minds are quite chatty and yours will want to keep talking even though you're trying to quiet it down. As you notice thoughts arising, just let them pass, and go back to watching your breathing. Eventually that mind chatter will quiet.

Another meditation technique you can use if you're worried or upset about your financial situation is to focus your attention on your Prosperity Picture. Sit in front of your Picture and direct your attention toward it. Recall how the individual images make you feel—actually feel these positive emotions and notice where in your body you feel them. Luxuriate here for several minutes. As you recall these yummy feelings you'll coax yourself out of the negative space and into a positive one. If you're really focused and feeling the positive energy of your Prosperity Picture, you'll push out the negative emotions . . . there's not room for both to occur at once.

You can also focus your attention on a mantra, which is a phrase, word, or sound you say over and over in your mind. Some use words such as "peace," "love," "one," or "calm." Try meditating with your own mantra—just keep repeating a word, phrase, or sound that makes you feel good. As your mind wanders, gently bring your focus back to your mantra. Some people prefer to look at an object or a candle flame. Others go on a visualization journey in which they picture a location that is peaceful and calm. You can also use guided visualizations to help you through this process.

You might also consider taking a meditation class. This can be quite helpful not only in learning to meditate but in developing a regular meditation practice. Ellen learned to meditate in a class she took along with her husband and mother. There was instruction and then four follow-up sessions. This support was very important for her, as the first few days of the meditation actually made her feel really cranky. As others in the group were sharing how they felt peaceful and calm, she reported feeling nauseous and achy. Ellen thinks it was years of stress leaving her body. Without the support of her teacher, she likely would have quit then and there. Instead, she kept practicing and now wouldn't go a day without meditating.

Many people experience practicing yoga as a type of moving meditation—a way to link the body, the breath, and the mind. As with deep breathing exercises and meditation, studies have found yoga to be effective in reducing stress, anxiety, and depression.

Yoga is also a beautiful metaphor for a balanced approach to money. If you've ever been to a yoga class, you know the instructor will often direct you to keep your attention on your own mat and not to compare yourself to others in the class. No matter your level, you are in the perfect place. Hmm . . . what if we didn't compare our financial situations to those of others? When you work hard to keep up appearances, envy others' good fortunes, or feel judgmental about the way others spend their money, you are on a speedboat to Scare-City. It's easy to get shipwrecked there and hard to be rescued so you can feel better about your own money.

Balance is a concept that can help us succeed in financial management just as it does in yoga. Balance between spending and saving, between giving and receiving, between risk and reward is critical in handling your money. Balance as you move through various yoga poses is critical for success there as well. And distractions can throw you off in both scenarios too. In yoga class Ellen notices that when she's doing one-legged positions she always loses balance when her thinking is distracted—sometimes even by wondering how the woman next to her can raise her leg so high! Instead, when she focuses on one point in front of her, breathes deeply, and feels inside that she's growing tall and strong, she balances with ease. Similarly, focusing your attention on what others are doing with their money, worrying about the future, and spending recklessly can all lead to toppling your financial life on its head. But redirecting your focus inward and putting more time, attention, and practice into balancing your financial life can help make it stronger.

Get to "I Know I'll Be Okay"

If there were a welcome sign in the Prosperity Zone, it would say, "You Will Be Okay." Of course, you want to be more than "okay," but beginning with this as a baseline belief is huge in terms of financial confidence. Getting to this point will be different for everyone. It takes self-knowledge and financial action. Running the numbers is often only part of the equation. Internal awareness is also crucial.

What will it take for you to be confident in your financial future? This is a very personal question. Jackie might feel that as long as she has a roof over her head, she knows she'll be okay. She could incorporate that into her Prosperity Picture by working toward getting her mortgage paid off as soon as possible. Rhonda has always been focused on supporting herself rather than relying on anyone else—if she can continue to do that, she knows she'll be okay. Consequently, she's pursuing an advanced degree, keeps her résumé up-to-date, and maintains a strong network of business contacts. She has also made sure to have good disability insurance coverage in place and a healthy solutions fund in case she's unable to work or loses her job.

Some people answer the "When will I know I'm okay?"

question with a specific dollar amount. For example, if you're thinking, "If I have $1 million, I know I'll be okay," we invite you to explore this a little deeper. What would $1 million do for you? What does it represent? A number—even a big number—usually isn't the only thing that will make us feel secure. The other issue with this approach is that a number is a moving target. Your cost of living typically increases over time due to inflation, and $1 million today won't buy you as much thirty years from now. If you accrued $1 million thirty years ago, you'd need roughly $2,250,000 to buy the same things today—more than twice as much. We might not be able to do this math in our head, but at an intuitive level our heads understand that having a specific number doesn't guarantee we'll be okay. Even if you have a number that is well thought out, that doesn't mean it will really be adequate enough to make sure you'll actually *feel* okay. It's about what this number represents, not the actual number.

Let's explore what might really help you feel okay through a visualizing process.

Sit in a comfortable position, in a quiet space where you will be uninterrupted for a few minutes. Take in a deep breath through your nose and exhale slowly through your mouth. Continue taking in three to five more deep breaths, and with each inhale feel yourself becoming more relaxed. With each exhale, feel yourself letting go of any stress or negative thoughts that are clinging to you. Know you can handle these at a later time.

From this relaxed state, observe yourself feeling totally relaxed and confident. Notice a feeling of calm in your body. Feel grounded. Feel confident. Imagine from this space that you *know* you will always be okay financially. Ask yourself, "What will help me feel okay?" Listen for the answer. Don't worry if you don't hear it right away. Again from a place of calm, clarity, and trust, ask, "How will I be okay? What will happen to ensure I'll always be okay?" Sit for a few more moments feeling the peace that comes along with this knowledge. Notice what this confidence feels like in your body. If doubt arises, that's fine and natural. Just let any thoughts of worry or doubt float past you and return to the feeling of knowing you will always be okay.

Now slowly and gently bring your attention back to the present moment. Take a couple of minutes to grab your Prosperity Notebook and write down any thoughts, ideas, and inspirations that came to you during this process.

Stop Financial Information Overload

Turning off the TV is a quick way to dial down financial stress. The media makes a lot of money by giving viewers conflicting information and "disasterizing" situations. It gets our attention because our brains are actually wired to give priority to bad news—as humans evolved, we needed to be alert to potential dangers as a way to protect ourselves from physical threats. All of this makes it easy to obsess about challenging situations.

Yes, it's good to be informed. But spending too much time watching sensationalized financial media not only raises your blood pressure, it can also actually hurt your investment returns. Dr. Richard Thaler of the University of Chicago found that people who ingested more financial news actually had lower investment returns than those who took in less news.

In one experiment, Thaler had people manage a fictional college endowment made up of two mutual funds. The subjects could choose how frequently they received information and how often they traded. Over a simulated twenty-five-year period, the experiment results were surprising. Participants who received information and had the opportunity to make trades only once every five years had more than twice the investment returns as the participants who received updates and had the opportunity to make trades once a month! Now, we're not saying you should watch the financial news and look at your accounts only every five years, but we are saying to be cautious of the amounts and sources of financial information you consume. More isn't necessarily better.

Our suggestion? Go on a media diet. Commit to limiting your TV news consumption for a short time and see how you feel. Perhaps you get your news fix from an online or print source that allows you to be more discriminating about what you are ingesting. Try it—we bet you won't miss the sensational news one bit.

Clear Clutter

When the markets are volatile and the economy is rocky, it's easy to feel out of control. We can't control these outside forces, but we can control how we react to them. When you're feeling out of control, one of the best things you can do is to create order around you. Lisa travels for work a great deal and is often at the mercy of airline schedules, weather delays, and other factors beyond her control. One of her tactics for dealing with the travel demands is to keep her handbag organized, to unpack and put her suitcase away as soon as she gets home, and to sort through the mail pile as quickly as possible after her trips. Though these things have absolutely no direct impact on her travel schedule, they calm her down. (When things get really stressful, she can be found alphabetizing the spice rack, but that's another story.)

Clearing clutter can also work for your money. While it's not a traditional financial strategy, it can be a powerful one because it has the potential to bring you a sense of calm and clarity. We're talking about two types of clutter: physical clutter, such as the endless paperwork, statements, and the like, and mental clutter, such as things we've done that we wish we hadn't or things we know we should do that we haven't yet. Once messes are cleaned up, you're likely to feel renewed mental capacity.

If you're like most people, you receive mounds of statements, canceled checks, insurance documents, and marketing material on a regular basis. In addition, you probably juggle other important papers, such as trust and power of attorney documents, home and auto ownership papers, and tax returns, to name a few. Without a system for reviewing and filing information, you can feel as if you're drowning in a sea of papers. This kind of clutter not only feels bad, it limits your prosperity. Every time you worry about what's in the pile on your desk or the envelopes stuffed in your drawers, you aren't focusing on what you want to *create*.

Need other reasons to get organized? It can find you real money. People can actually lose track of their investments, and millions of dollars are turned over to states each year from unclaimed accounts.

Remember Kathleen from Chapter Two, who found a $500,000 investment she didn't realize she had until she got organized? Now, this might not be typical, but—wow! Even 1 percent of this would be well worth looking for. Another woman, Katie, attended one of our workshops and sent Ellen a letter a week later that said this: "Imagine my delight and my amazement at the following *non-coincidence*. I had just emptied out my T-shirt drawer and was separating the 'keep' vs. 'donate' when a *wad* of $20 bills fell out of one of the T-shirts! $700 to be exact. How's that for a 'sign' that I was on the right track in terms of decluttering!"

There are also practical reasons to create financial order in your life. Having a well-organized financial system will be immensely helpful if the IRS ever comes knocking at your door. If you can quickly and easily provide them with the information they want to see, it will be a less stressful experience. Similarly, if something happens to you, having orderly finances will make it easier for your family members or friends to find your important documents. Don't make your loved ones forget they miss you when you're gone because they are so ticked off that you've made it difficult for them to settle your affairs!

Here are some ideas for putting your documents in order:

• Use a safe-deposit box. If you don't already have one, consider getting a safe-deposit box. As a general rule, only documents and items that are difficult or impossible to replace need to be kept in a safe-deposit box. Examples include: adoption papers, automobile titles, birth certificates, coin or stamp collections, valuable jewelry, and deeds and titles.
• Inventory your home. We suggest you make an inventory of the contents of your home for insurance purposes. This should be supported by a video or pictures. It's important that you store a copy of the video or pictures in the cloud or somewhere outside your home. Then place a backup in your safe-deposit box.

It's also a good idea to make a list of your important documents and note the location of where they are all kept (e.g., safe-deposit box, file cabinet in the basement, file in your office, etc.). You can use the document list included in the Chapter Four Appendix as a guide. This will be invaluable in the event that something happens to you. Make sure to note your advisors, attorneys, accountants, and other professionals on the list, as well as how to find your log-in IDs and passwords, and where your safe-deposit box—and key—is located. Put a copy of the list in the safe-deposit box, and give a copy to a trusted family member or friend.

After Ellen's father passed away, she was initially unable to find her parents' tax returns. She looked through cabinets where her dad had stored financial statements and drawers where he kept canceled checks, but they were nowhere to be found. Eventually, Ellen happened to look through the desk drawer in the guest bedroom, where she discovered a listing of all her parents' important documents. She had given her father a locator sheet to complete and didn't realize he had actually filled it out. Turns out the tax returns were in an old file cabinet in the back of the basement—not a place Ellen had even considered checking. So when you complete the important documents listing make sure to let someone know where *that* document is!

Here are some other suggestions for creating financial order in your life:

• Start sorting as soon as you receive paperwork and marketing material so that it doesn't continue to pile up. Discard any material you don't intend to act upon right away.
• Set up a system for filing paperwork. This can be as simple as a three-ring binder or file folders in an accordion file. This will not only free up space and reduce stress, but also may assist you in catching errors in your accounts. Errors don't happen often; however, money can be withdrawn from the wrong person's account

and fees can be charged in error. In most cases, you can shred monthly and quarterly statements after you receive your year-end statement. Consider going paperless and getting e-statements. Get a good electronic filing system so that you can access these when you need them and make sure you regularly back up your computer.

• Establish a system for bill paying. Many people pay bills twice a month. Others write the check to pay a bill when it arrives and note its due date next to the stamp on the envelope as a reminder to mail their payment. To avoid stamps altogether, online bill paying is an easy, efficient alternative.

• Streamline your accounts. Do you have too many similar accounts in various places for no practical reason? You're not alone. If there is no logical reason to maintain multiple accounts, close some of them. Streamlining your accounts can help reduce paper-work and may reduce administrative fees.

• Take charge of unfinished financial responsibilities. Check back on your assessment from Chapter Two and commit to taking care of the financial to-dos on your list. Whenever there is a financial task you haven't done yet but know you should, you're creating an energy leak for yourself. You're focusing attention on what has not been completed, rather than on more productive things, whether you're aware of it or not. Don't underestimate the negative impact of mental clutter.

Weather the Financial Downturns

The economy and financial markets are cyclical. There are times of expansion and times of contraction. And here's an interesting thing: contraction isn't always bad.

Being from Chicago, we are no strangers to long winters. By midwinter we've gotten used to gray skies, sooty slush, and subzero temperatures that freeze your eyelashes. People walk through the streets bundled up, hunched over, and looking down to avoid the wind blowing in their faces. What keeps us going—and not moving to a warmer location like sensible people—is knowing that spring always comes! Some years it takes longer than others, but it always comes and, boy, do we feel good on that first day we can put on some flip-flops and see a tulip sprouting! And even though winter can be brutal, it offers its own kind of upside—it's a perfect excuse to light some candles, snuggle up with a blanket, and binge watch a TV series on Netflix, or wear that super cute heavy sweater that makes you sweat if it's too warm outside. Lisa secretly relishes an excuse to be a couch potato once in a while—she's inspired by her friend Mike, a former Chicagoan who spent the entire last holiday season calling himself "Elf on the Couch" instead of the popular children's toy Elf on the Shelf!

This is the case with economic cycles as well. Things will get better—historically they always have. We can't control when the economy will turn around, but we can control how we react to the circumstances and make adjustments. In tight economic times, creativity and resourcefulness are beautiful traits to possess. Use these opportunities to take a fresh look at your spending. When finances are flush, most people are freer with how they spend money. They tend to be less careful and discriminating. This can be fun and less stressful to be sure, but can also lead to waste and unconscious expenditures.

In the last big downturn, Ellen's friend Laurie looked at all of the expenses in her law firm. She realized the firm was spending thousands of dollars on publications that no one ever read. She found cabinets full of supplies that the firm continually ordered but no one seemed to use, and she discovered that few people were actually using the coffee service they paid for. This money was being wasted for years, but it took the downturn for anyone to realize it.

On a more personal note, when Lisa's husband, who runs his own business, was coming up to the possible end of a long-term client contract, the two of them sat down to take a hard look at their monthly expenditures in anticipation of a potential cash flow shift. They found they were both paying for online Weight Watchers access that they rarely used (don't ask . . .), two individual digital subscriptions to the *New York Times* when they could share one, a monthly DVR fee they didn't need because they had changed their electronics setup, and a gym membership for Lisa that she also rarely used because she works out at hotel gyms when she travels and runs outside. They corrected all of that for a total savings of $131 a month. Remember our earlier discussion of compound interest? Well, this $131 invested monthly and earning a hypothetical 5 percent interest could grow to be more than $20,000 in ten years. That's way more fun than feeling guilty about a gym membership not being used!

In Chapter Two we talked about having a spending plan so you can know what money flows in and out of your household. This information is super helpful to prepare you for any changes that may come your way because you'll be more easily able to assess whether you're spending money on things you truly value. You'll also have a much easier time making adjustments if your financial situation changes and have the insight you need to be more flexible.

*When the Storm Is Coming, Put Your Money Where
Your Mouth (and Value System) Is*

Does how you spend your money reflect what is truly important to you? To get a clear handle on this, we recommend taking your spending plan from Chapter Two to the next level by overlaying it with a values component. Start with your summary of where you're spending money and evaluate each category. Then decide whether your values are being expressed in the way you spend. For instance, if education is something you greatly value and you plan to help pay for your kids' college costs, are you allocating enough money toward saving for this goal? Our friend Brigit told us she wanted to make sure her daughter Ana could graduate from college debt free. In order to make sure there was enough money for Ana's education, Brigit would need to save about $750 per month. At the time, she was saving only about $80 per month. But when she looked at her spending plan, she realized she was spending an extra $60 monthly on premium cable and $55 on lunches out during the week, neither of which was particularly important to her. She decided to cut back on her cable plan and bring lunch to work three days a week. By focusing on her values, Brigit was able to reallocate more than $200 per month toward her savings goal. This still isn't enough to get her to her full savings goal, but she'll be much closer to helping Ana graduate from college debt free.

Is making a difference in the world important to you? If so, have you included an allocation for financial donations to causes you care about in your spending plan? We talked about this in Chapter Four, but it's worth reminding ourselves that intentionally earmarking cash for gifts to others is a great example of how to align your spending with your values. It's also a way to loosen your grip on money. When you're focused on helping others less fortunate than yourself, it helps you move away from fear-based Scare-City thoughts and land solidly in the Prosperity Zone. An attitude of abundance will serve you well in all economies—especially challenging ones.

What if My Financial Fears Become Debilitating?

Speaking of challenges, an important part of self-soothing is to have a strategy ready and waiting for those really serious bouts of worry that we all inevitably face from time to time. We're talking those mother lode/death spirals of worry here. Ever catch yourself falling into one of those? It goes something like this: "Oh, my gosh—I got a low score on my annual review at work. What if I lose my job? And then I can't pay my bills . . . and then I can't make my mortgage payment, and I lose my house, and my kids can't go to college and they turn to a life of crime, and then we all go to jail and then I am released but I'm a bag lady and I'll never get to wear nice shoes . . . !" Although you rationally know that this will never actually happen, it can be easy to get caught in one of these spirals.

So in times of high anxiety and worry, what can you do to feel better? Dr. Tim Ursiny, owner of Advantage Coaching & Training in West Chicago and a PhD in psychology, advocates a technique called "Truth Talk." It's based on cognitive approaches of psychology such as rational emotive behavior therapy, which teaches that unpleasant emotions are almost always caused by our perception of what occurs rather than what actually occurs. In the example above, the concern is not that you *have* lost your job, only that you're afraid that you might—but that possibility is frightening enough to cause serious anxiety. Most people eventually work through these situations and get to a calmer, more logical place, but that process can take lots of time and cause suffering along the way. Truth Talk, a four-step process, gets you there faster.

Step One: Ask yourself, "What happened?" You need to identify an actual fact, not a perception. So in the example above, the fact is that you got a low score on your annual review.

Step Two: Ask yourself, "What emotion am I feeling about it?" In this case, that's easy—it's fear! You're afraid for yourself and your family.

Step Three: Ask yourself, "What is my perception about the event that happened?" In other words, what are you "telling yourself" about it? In this example, you're telling yourself you're going to lose your job, your home, and more. Here's where it gets really interesting. There are two follow-up filter questions for this question:

Filter Question One: Am I certain that this perception is 100 percent true?

Filter Question Two: Does focusing on this perception help me?

If the answer to either one of the filter questions is no, you can be certain it's an irrational thought pattern. How? Well, if you're not certain it's 100 percent true, you don't know that it will happen—so it's irrational to think about it. If it is 100 percent true but thinking about it is not helpful and is causing you stress or anxiety, it's also irrational—because you're intentionally causing yourself needless anxiety. In either case, the goal is to stop the thought. But here's the thing: you can't just erase a thought. It's like the case of the pink elephant. If we ask you not to think about a pink elephant, you have no choice but to think of a pink elephant—the opposite of what you want. So rather than erase the thought, the goal is to replace it.

Step Four: Find a way to replace your initial emotion with one that is positive and helpful. This may not be easy, but you can do it. In this example, you might replace the emotion of fear with gratitude. "I'm grateful because I've gotten a warning that something is wrong at work and now I have a chance to fix it." Or you may focus on gratitude, but for a different reason. "I'm grateful because even if I do lose my job, I've still got my family and health, which is most important." You might choose to replace the feeling of fear with something entirely different, like excitement. "I'm excited because I've never really liked this job anyway and this will give me a chance to find something I enjoy." Or peace: "I feel calm, because it's just a job. If I lose it, I'll find a way to handle it." Maybe even empowerment: "I feel good because I know I'm strong and good at what I do. I will overcome this." Some of these alternatives may speak to you; some may not, and that's fine. There's obviously no one right answer, just what works for you at the time.

Dr. Ursiny likes to tell a great Truth Talk success story. He was just about to give a high-stakes presentation for one of his biggest corporate clients and was chatting with the attendees. A gentleman came up to him and said, "So, you're the coach for today, huh?" Tim smiled, introduced himself, and chatted for a moment, then excused himself. A few minutes later, he walked by the same guy and heard him say, "Yeah, I heard they're going to fire this coach." Tim was mortified—this was a really important client for him that meant a lot to his bottom line. Not only that, but he was just about to walk onstage and deliver a big presentation. He had to be on his game and he had to act fast. Here's how he used Truth Talk.

He identified a factual description of what happened: He heard an employee of an important client say the coach was going to be fired.

His emotion: Fear—big time!

His perception of the event: He was definitely going to be fired.

Filter Question One: Is he certain it's 100 percent true. No—this employee could have been gossiping or misinformed.

Filter Question Two: Does his perception help him? No—it hurts him. The answer to not just one but both questions is no. It's definitely an irrational thought.

Positive replacement thought: Tim chose gratitude—that he'd heard it in time to adjust and make sure he did a fantastic job with his presentation . . . which was starting in just minutes!

So with his new emotion of gratitude, he walked onstage and did, in fact, deliver a fabulous presentation—one of his best. Afterward, he decided to share his experience with the guy he had overheard talking. He went up and said, "Hey, I've just got to tell you—I heard you talking about 'firing the coach . . .'" The guy looked at him and replied, "Yeah, Indianapolis sucks this year. I heard they're looking for a new head coach."

Oh, the stories we tell ourselves!

A word to the wise: this process takes practice. Our fear brain is not wired to handle things in this manner and will resist at first. Just like breathing control, meditation, and many of the other techniques in this chapter, it takes constant practice. But once you get into the swing of it, it holds huge promise to alleviate stress and make a dent in your anxiety levels.

Lean on Your Team During the Tough Times

Another tactic to manage financial worry is to have people available to help you. We all spend time now and then worrying about things that never happen. It's so easy to play out a scenario in your mind that has no basis in reality. Or perhaps it does—maybe there really is some cause for concern. Wouldn't having a plan help in either situation? Regular financial check-ins with a professional advisor can help you stay connected with reality. Knowing the real implications of your financial situation is much better than burying your head in the sand, hoping for the best, but also fearing the worst.

Cindy was so embarrassed and scared about her financial situation she was paralyzed. Early in her career as a Web designer, she did contract work for a large company. Although brilliant and talented at her work, she was inexperienced at running a business and didn't realize she was required to reserve some of her income for taxes. She spent her consulting income and when April 15 rolled around she found out she owned the IRS $38,000, which she didn't have. She hired an accountant, who tried to work this out for her. As she tells the story, "He judged me, and advised me to pursue a strategy I knew intuitively would cause bigger issues with the IRS. I told him this but he didn't listen. I ended up having a lien put on my bank account and the IRS taking all of the small amount I had managed to save." The next year, still not having money to pay taxes, she avoided filing a tax return altogether. She did the same thing the next year and the next. Understandably, Cindy had a difficult time growing her business. She lived in constant fear that the IRS would take whatever she earned. She felt incredible shame about her situation. Cindy is really smart but ended up in a situation that made her feel stupid.

When she finally called Ellen for advice, she said, "The terror and worry finally got so great that it outweighed my shame about the situation." Calmly listening, Ellen realized that what Cindy needed was a smart and nonjudgmental accountant to help her move ahead.

Within forty-five minutes, Ellen called an accountant she thought would be a good fit for Cindy, Cindy contacted the accountant, and she was on the path to getting out of a bad situation.

It's tempting to get judgy about Cindy not filing her taxes, but most of us have avoided something somewhere along the line that we knew we should've taken care of. It might not be as dramatic as this, but we all have things we could do better. If you find yourself stuck, confused, or really worried, consider reaching out to someone to help. You might have to try a few times to find the right assistance, but the right person is out there for you. You can even put an image representing the ideal support on your Prosperity Picture.

Having a strong team of professionals as well as supportive friends and family will help you move through difficult situations with more ease, clarity, and wisdom.

Put a Safety Net Under Your Plan

Some of the risk to your financial situation can be protected through the use of insurance. Whether the risk is that you or your partner might become ill, disabled, or die, or that something bad might happen to something you own, like a house or car, insurance can cushion the blow. Through paying premiums to your insurance companies, you are sharing the potential risk.

We know this isn't a new idea for most of you. Most of us are familiar with the basic types of insurance and they all play an essential role in protecting you and your family financially. If you're not well covered in any one of these areas, we encourage you to rectify the situation immediately—there's too much at stake not to.

Health insurance: Let's begin with the all-important area of health insurance, which really is nonnegotiable. You need it, period. If for any reason you don't have a plan in place, please make this your number one priority! Look into government-funded options, employer-sponsored plans, or private insurance. The last thing you want to do is find yourself in a position where you or your family members have an expensive or ongoing health need that you can't cover. We've been to more than a few fund-raising events for individuals who have been victims of auto accidents, diagnosed with cancer, or faced lifelong disease and had either inadequate or nonexistent health insurance. It goes without saying that in addition to the incredible difficulty and emotional devastation these kinds of health events involve, being underinsured or not insured at all can lead to financial devastation as well. If you have some insurance but aren't sure it's adequate, pick up the phone and call your insurance agent. If you don't have insurance at all, get yourself in front of a computer as soon as you possibly can and visit HealthCare.gov or the Obamacare site for your specific state.

Auto insurance: Approximately 15 percent of Americans don't have car insurance. Not only is this illegal in all fifty states, it's also an example of something that could cripple you financially if you need it but don't have it. If you don't qualify for or can't afford auto insurance, you're better off not driving. Seriously. Take public transportation, walk, bike, do whatever it takes, but do not operate a vehicle. If you already have auto insurance, take the time to make sure that your policy is current and adequately covers you.

Home insurance: If you own a home, homeowner's insurance will cover the replacement cost of your belongings and the rebuilding of the structure in the case of loss. If you have a mortgage on your house, lenders require you to have homeowner's insurance, but even if your home is paid off, this is nonnegotiable. Just like health and auto insurance, you need to have it to protect yourself. If you're a renter, you need renter's insurance to cover the replacement cost of your belongings in the case of loss. (The apartment owner assumes responsibility for the structure.) Roughly two thirds of all renters don't have insurance, which is troubling when you think how much it would cost to replace all of your belongings in the case of loss. It's even more troubling when you look at how affordable renter's insurance can be—the average renter's policy costs less than $200 a year.

Umbrella insurance: This is extra liability protection over and above what you have through your auto and homeowner's policies. This type of insurance can help protect your assets in the event of an accident determined to be your fault, if someone gets hurt on your property and sues you for damages, or in other situations in which you may be held liable. The rule of thumb is that you should have umbrella insurance equal to your net worth. Your auto and homeowner's or renter's insurance will contain some liability insurance, so the goal is to use umbrella insurance to fill in any gap between what your existing policies contain and what your net worth is.

Life insurance: If someone is dependent on your income or if you're dependent on theirs, and if there wouldn't be enough assets to live on if a death took that income away, you probably need life insurance. If not, you might not need it, but may have other reasons for wanting it, such as to provide an extra cushion to your family, to cover estate taxes, or to make a larger donation to a charity after you're gone. Safety tip: if someone is dependent on your income or if you're dependent on someone else's income and you're not 100 percent sure that enough life insurance is in place in either scenario, go find out! There's no shortage of stories about widows who find out that their husbands were uninsured or underinsured after their husbands have passed away. By then it's too late. Some of these people have found themselves losing houses, not sure how to pay the basic monthly bills, and worse. Don't let yourself or someone you love be one of them.

Disability insurance: If you get sick or suffer an injury that makes it impossible for you to work and bring in an income, disability insurance will provide you with a portion of your salary—typically around 60 percent. Think you'll never really need this type of insurance? Well, we certainly hope you don't, but consider this: 64 percent of wage earners believe they have a 2 percent or less chance of being disabled for at least three months or more during their working career. Yet the actual odds of this happening for a worker entering the workforce today are about *25 percent*. If you think social security would help out if you became disabled, you should know that two thirds of initial claims are denied. So if you can't afford to live without your income, consider getting disability insurance. If it's offered by your employer, sign up for the biggest benefit you can. If your employer doesn't offer it, consider buying it on your own.

Long-term care insurance: If your health declines to a point where you can't care for yourself, this insurance helps to cover the cost of care, either at home, in a nursing home, or in an assisted-living facility. If you have a partner, having this kind of protection for them is just as important. Long-term care costs can be very expensive. You may have done wonderful financial planning, but if you or your partner needs long-term care, the costs can cause financial trauma. If you have parents you may need to support in the event of a prolonged illness, you'll want to encourage them to look at long-term care. We know people who have chosen to buy long-term care insurance for their parents because they see it as a more affordable way to help their parents than potentially covering their institutional care in the future.

Remember it's critical to review all your insurance policies annually to make sure you're protected properly. Take some time to go through them now or commit to yourself a time when you can do it. Taking an inventory of your insurance will help you think through the pertinent details which can be beneficial in and of itself.

Insurance can be confusing. If you are unclear of what you have, what it covers or whether it's adequate, ask for help. Contact your benefits department at work, the insurance companies who cover you, or your insurance agent to get smart and to get secure that you have what you need.

You Don't Have to Be Rich Like Jed Clampett to Need an Estate Plan

Being financially resilient means protecting not just yourself but also those you love, and an estate plan is one important way to do this. Estate plans are not just for the über-rich (if Jed Clampett means nothing to you, think Richie Rich or Tony Stark). The main purpose of having an estate plan is to make sure the people and causes that are important to you are provided for after you're gone. Estate planning is fertile ground for procrastination—people drag their feet on this (understandably so), yet it's so important for your loved ones. Here are some basics to consider:

A will: This is a legal document that outlines how you would like your property to be distributed and provides for the care of any minor children. If you die without a will (a state of affairs known as "intestate," which sounds vaguely dirty but is not), there's no guarantee that your property will go to the people you want to have it or that your kids will be taken care of by whom you would like. Without a will, the state will decide how your assets are distributed according to a set formula and will appoint someone to care for your children.

A revocable living trust: This is a complex-sounding phrase that refers to a straightforward document that authorizes someone to handle your property. It's set up while you are alive, hence the "living" in living trust. It's revocable because while you are alive and competent to do so, you can make changes. These trusts typically become irrevocable after you die, meaning nobody else can change them. It's common to be the trustee of your own trust while you are able to handle your own affairs. In the trust you'll list the people you want to step in and help manage your financial life if you are unable to do so on your own. These documents also allow your heirs to avoid the probate process after you die, which can save lots of time and money.

A durable power of attorney: This is a legal document authorizing someone to manage your affairs on your behalf. You'll need to name the people who will make medical and financial decisions for you if you can't. Think of them as your lieutenants or seconds in command.

For medical issues, a power of attorney names a person to make medical decisions for you and spells out your wishes for life support. The person you name should be someone you're confident will follow through on your wishes. Being clear about how you want these issues handled is one of the kindest things you can do for the person in this role. Imagine how incredibly difficult it would be in the first place to have to make life-and-death decisions about someone you love, and how much harder it would be if you weren't sure what they really wanted.

Similarly, you'll need to designate someone as having power of attorney for your property. This person will handle your financial and other material affairs if you are unable to do so. This includes everything from making sure your home is maintained and paying monthly bills all the way to making major decisions about whether to sell property and other business-related affairs.

Designated beneficiaries: Some of your accounts, such as 401(k) plans, IRAs, annuities, and life insurance, will pass directly to your heirs by designating a beneficiary. Do you know whom you've listed on these accounts? Have you designated a contingent beneficiary? A contingent beneficiary is next in line if the primary beneficiary dies before you. Review your beneficiaries at least every few years. It's quite common for people to forget to change their beneficiaries after a divorce. If you don't want your ex to inherit your account, make sure to get that beneficiary designation changed.

Got Kids?

Do you have children? This is one of the most compelling reasons to get your affairs in order. If the kids have another living parent or guardian, in most cases that person would legally assume the responsibility for their care. But what if they don't? Or can't? Or what if both of you passed away? If you have minor children, you need to think through these possibilities and decide who would take over.

And, of course, you also need to make sure the designated legal guardian would have a way to pay for their care. Do you have enough assets to pass along to him or her so that the cost of raising your children would be covered? Many people use life insurance for this purpose.

If you have assets you want to pass on to your kids, you'll also want to appoint someone to be a trustee to handle the money for them until they are old enough or responsible enough to do this on their own. This may or may not be the same person you designated as the guardian for their care. As they're choosing a guardian, most parents do their best to pick someone who would be likely to raise the kids in alignment with how they are raising them. For the person in charge of the money, you want to choose a responsible, trustworthy person who understands money and would act in the best financial interest of the kids.

In some situations, it makes sense to have a trustee even for grown children. This would typically occur if you have reason to believe that your grown child or other beneficiary might not be able to handle his or her own affairs responsibly. The trustee can be an individual or a corporate trustee (often a bank). Why would someone designate a corporate trustee? Perhaps you don't have a responsible person in your life to designate. Corporate trustees can be expensive, so this route makes sense only when the estate is large enough or the situation complicated enough to warrant the expense.

We know a woman, Susie, who inherited more than $5 million after her father died. Sadly, she had substance abuse issues and her father hadn't designated a trustee to help her manage the money. It wasn't a pretty picture. Although Susie had an attorney helping to settle her father's estate, she didn't sign or file the tax forms on a timely basis and had to pay hundreds of thousands of dollars to the government in penalties. She also spent much more than she could afford, got involved in several business deals that ended badly, and even had money stolen from her outright. Within ten years almost all of the money was gone. Her story could have been much happier if her father had assigned a responsible person or institution to help manage the money for her.

Also, spend some time thinking about how you want to make a difference in the world after you're gone. Is there a cause or organization you want to support? Leaving a legacy isn't just for the ultrawealthy. Naming a charitable organization in your will or trust or as a beneficiary of your life insurance or retirement account can not only make a big impact for a cause important to you, but also possibly save your heirs taxes.

It's a lot to think through. Some people choose to create their own estate plan using templates available online. If you have a more complicated situation, or are not confident in your ability to execute the proper documents correctly, we highly recommend that you hire a good estate planning attorney to guide you through this process. Attorneys can walk you through these questions, help minimize tax obligations for your heirs, and make sure your plan is legally sound.

We've covered a whole lot of territory concerning your financial resilience. Just as the little pig who built his house out of bricks put in more effort than his piggy brothers and ended up with a house the big bad wolf couldn't blow down, spending time building your financial foundation from the inside out will serve you well.

Gain Traction Through Action

• Shift your perspective to deal with challenges. Move out of Scare-City and into the Prosperity Zone by asking yourself the "Find the Upside in a Down Situation" questions in this chapter. Note your responses in your Prosperity Notebook.

• Breathe! The next time you find yourself fretting about money or another problem in your life, take a few moments to take some deep, cleansing breaths. Your stress level will lower and your body will thank you.

• Develop a regular stress reduction practice. Try meditation or yoga as a way to neutralize your financial and life stress. The positive effects can be amazing!

• Get to "I know I'll be okay." Reflect on what it really means to you personally to "feel okay" about your money. Use the visualization exercise in this chapter to help you clarify what it looks and feels like to know you'll be okay.

• Go on a media diet. Reduce your exposure to TV, print, and online news and see whether your state of mind improves.

• Clear clutter. Increase your sense of clarity and calm by clearing your financial clutter. Get yourself a safe-deposit box, inventory your home and important documents (see list in Chapter Four), create systems for filing paperwork and paying bills, and address those nagging unfinished financial responsibilities.

• Check to see whether you have "misplaced" any investments. Visit MissingMoney.com, or the designated Web site for your state, to search for unclaimed property.

• Create a values-based spending plan. Is your spending aligned with your values? Are there opportunities to reduce or eliminate unnecessary expenses and reallocate that money to saving or spending in areas you value more?

- Use Truth Talk. The next time you're feeling extreme worry and anxiety, try practicing Truth Talk to neutralize it as quickly as possible.

- Lean on your team. You don't have to face financial fears and challenges alone. Trusted, knowledgeable friends and financial professionals can provide advice and perspective to help creatively work toward your ideal outcomes.

- Put a safety net under your finances. Make sure you have proper auto, home, health, life, umbrella, and long-term care insurance in place and that you understand the coverage you have.

- Have an up-to-date estate plan. Do this for the people you love!

Chapter Seven

Step Seven: Build a Lifetime of Prosperity

We've been on quite a journey together. In just six chapters we've covered a lot of ground, and we're almost done. But we've saved the best for last! Just as you can't see the view from the top of the mountain without going through the work to climb it, you can't see the possibilities for your own resources and their potential impact on the world without going through a financial building process. At this point we've walked you through the process starting from base camp and provided you with the right tools and direction to guide you toward your financial summit. The summit we're talking about is a shift from focusing on the "one" in money to the "we" in wealth. When you're able to see your resources as a means to better not only your life but also your world, you give yourself the chance to create and experience true prosperity.

Yes, we've already talked about the benefits of generosity and giving in Chapter Five, but as you recall, those benefits were mostly centered around you—if you give, you are likely to be healthier, you'll potentially be more successful in your work, and you may feel a greater sense of happiness. And, of course, you are helping others in the process. Though wonderful to experience and highly desirable, these benefits are really just the start. We're going to delve into something even bigger and more meaningful in this final chapter. We are talking here about seeing your money as a reflection of your purpose in life. How you use it, the impact you make with it, and the influence you wield with it can practically and energetically support you in creating an extraordinary life—for yourself and for those in your orbit!

We are holding this space for you to play big with your money—well beyond what is typically talked about when it comes to women and finances. Why not become more than just smart about money and set your sights on becoming *wise*? Wise in ways that open you to the possibility of managing and using your resources for the highest good in your life. Wise in ways that guide you to "make change" with your money. This type of shift in perspective is quite possibly the most meaningful adjustment you can make in your financial life. And one that can add even more significance, passion, and purpose to your Prosperity Picture.

Women as Change Makers

We see women as having a unique power to be true "change makers," and we aren't alone in this vision. At the 2009 Vancouver Peace Summit, the Dalai Lama said something a bit unexpected and quite inspiring. He declared, "The world will be saved by the Western woman." Wow—this really sets the stage for us to play big in the world, huh? At the moment he said it, he was standing onstage next to Mairead Corrigan Maguire and Betty Williams, both peace activists from Northern Ireland and recipients of the Nobel Peace Prize; Mary Robinson, former president of Ireland and

UN High Commissioner for Human Rights; and Jody Williams, an American political activist focused on banning land mines and also a Nobel Peace Prize recipient. Perhaps he was influenced by the amazing female company he was keeping at the moment! The Dalai Lama has also said on numerous occasions that he inherited his compassion from his mother and that he believes women, with their nurturing instinct, are "naturally compassionate."

Research bears out this idea. There's growing evidence that women business owners across the globe are more likely to reinvest their profits in education, their family, and their community. The work of Muhammad Yunus and the Grameen Bank shows not only that microcredit loans given to women in emerging countries are nearly always paid back, but also that those funds are likely to be used to invest back in businesses that help educate children and lift families out of poverty. *New York Times* columnist Nicholas Kristof and Sheryl WuDunn sum it up neatly by pointing out, "There's a growing recognition among everyone from the World Bank to the U.S. military's Joint Chiefs of Staff to aid organizations like CARE that focusing on women and girls is the most effective way to fight global poverty and extremism. That's why foreign aid is increasingly directed to women. The world is awakening to a powerful truth: Women and girls aren't the problem; they're the solution."

What makes all this even more exciting is that women across the globe are positioned to control more money than ever before. It's estimated that as much as $59 trillion will transfer between generations over the next forty years. It is projected that 70 percent of that money will end up in the hands of women, because they are statistically more likely to outlive their husbands and brothers. Estimates vary, but we're talking about $28 trillion to $41 trillion that women are likely to control in the next forty years. At the risk of stating the obvious, this is an enormous number! Even if we use the low end of this range and round down, it means $25 trillion is likely to transfer into the control of women. How much is $25 trillion? It's 25 with twelve zeroes after it. If you laid one trillion dollar bills end to end they would measure 96,906,566 miles. That's more than enough to reach the sun. Speaking of which, $25 trillion could get you more than twelve round-trips there!

This enormous number gets us dreaming . . . women as change makers with economic might to back them up. What if just 1 percent of this money were used for making the world a better place? What could happen? For a start, every child on the planet could have an education and world hunger could be ended. Mind-boggling, but true! And what if we went further? If just 10 percent of that $25 trillion were used as a force for good in the world, we could also:

- eliminate most major infectious diseases worldwide
- increase research into renewable energy by 1,000 percent
- increase research for autism, breast cancer, and Alzheimer's by 1,000 percent
- increase funding to end human trafficking by 1,000 percent
- . . . and we would still have enough left over to set up an investment fund that would generate enough interest to continue to pay for all these initiatives on an ongoing basis

You might be thinking, "That's very nice, but I'm not inheriting anything!" That's true for many people, but will you possibly be leaving an inheritance? Do you have the ability to make a difference today with your money? No matter where you are in your financial life, as Anne Frank said, "How wonderful it is that nobody need wait a single moment before starting to improve the world."

As these trillions of dollars transfer into the hands of women, the possibilities are truly beautiful!

Don't misunderstand our intent here—we like boys too! There are amazing men all over the planet making a difference. We're simply pointing out that if you're a woman you may have a unique or as yet unrecognized power to make the world a better place. And it's amazingly inspiring to know women across the street and across the globe are stepping into their economic power in this incredible fashion.

Your Prosperity Echo

From your vantage point atop your personal "financial summit," consider that your good, kind, and generous acts not only directly support the people you're assisting, but quite often reverberate out to many more people than you realize. Here's an example of what we mean: Chicago-based nonprofit One Million Degrees helps low-income community college students earn degrees through a combination of financial support, skill building, and mentorship. Formerly known as the Illinois Education Foundation, the organization changed its name to One Million Degrees because the founders and directors were beginning to see that the degrees these students were earning were having an impact not just on their own lives as individuals, but on many other people's lives well beyond what anyone had initially thought. Students in the program often overcome incredible obstacles to become the first ones in their families and circles of friends to attend college. When they make that kind of decision, and ultimately get their degrees, they inspire siblings, friends, and other family members to do the same. Not only that, but after earning their degrees, it's much easier for them to find higher-paying jobs, which in turn makes it easier for them to support their own children and encourage them to go to college, and so on and so on. The "echo" is enormous, so much so that the organization's mission is now to put college degrees into the hands of so many people that they will ultimately touch one million lives. We believe they'll touch many more than that.

As a reader of this book and, hopefully, an ambassador of some of the ideas it contains, you are now in a position to lead and encourage others to do the same thing. Perhaps you'll sit down with your son or daughter and help them establish their own investment account as a tool to understand money in a deeper way, as Cheryl in Chicago did. Or maybe you'll point out how important it is to establish an estate plan or a long-term-care insurance policy to a friend who doesn't have one. It might be that people who travel in your circles will simply see you approaching your money and life goals differently and start down a similar path without your ever knowing about it.

Playing BIG

The Prosperity Picture you created in Chapter One is a glimpse into what's really important to you. We are willing to bet that if you take a look at your Picture right now, you'll see within it at least one or two ideas that have the potential to make a huge impact, not just on your life and not just on the lives of those you care about and touch, but also on the lives of people you haven't even met yet, and even for some you may never meet!

Perhaps you are familiar with the work of Marianne Williamson.

Marianne is a spiritual advisor and the bestselling author of multiple books, including *A Return to Love,* in which appears a popular quote:

> *Our deepest fear is not that we are inadequate. Our deepest fear is that we are powerful beyond measure. It is our light, not our darkness that most frightens us. We ask ourselves, Who am I to be brilliant, gorgeous, talented, fabulous? Actually, who are you not to be? . . . Your playing small does not serve the world. There is nothing enlightened about shrinking so that other people won't feel insecure around you. We are all meant to shine, as children do . . . And as we let our own light shine, we unconsciously give other people permission to do the same. As we are liberated from our own fear, our presence automatically liberates others.*

A wonderful woman at Lisa's church gave her a printout of this quote sometime around 2002. She instinctively liked it and hung it on her refrigerator. (If you haven't noticed by now, we're big on hanging things on the refrigerator.) One day as she looked at it, she had a sort of revelation. In a moment of clarity, focus, and self-connection, she realized this: she didn't really understand what the hell it meant! Seriously. Parts of it seemed clear enough, but it didn't seem feasible to her that she could actually be "powerful beyond measure," and even if she could, she didn't see why she would necessarily be frightened about that concept, or frightened of her "light."

But in the course of researching this book and talking with so many amazing people, she saw the quote starting to become clearer. Nicole is one of the people who helped provide clarity. She's a vibrant woman who is a wife and mother of five in New Jersey and a huge believer in giving back. She grew up in a family where philanthropy was valued. Her grandfather volunteered at the municipal fire house, she served as a candy striper at the local hospital at a young age, and her family provided financial support to those in need as much as they could. So it's only natural that philanthropic work is a top priority for her. Now, despite her demanding days as the mother of five children, Nicole continues to do charity work, which includes contributing significant time to Room to Read, an international organization that advocates for literacy and gender equality in Asia and Africa. Nicole lit up as she described the mission of the organization and how much she enjoys her role with them. She talked about how she "almost feels guilty because she enjoys doing the work so much," how it gives her a sense of purpose beyond her day-to-day life, and helps her feel she's doing what she was truly meant to do. Then she paused for a couple of moments, her demeanor shifted, and in a quieter voice that was somewhat tentative and accompanied by a slightly nervous chuckle, she said, "It's cool to give . . . This organization will change the world."

And there it was. That last bit. The last thing she said, the part that came across as something she conceivably might have forgotten about, is one of the most profound things any of us can ever say about anything: "This will change the world." This was Nicole's "light"! Her work with this organization is one example of how she personally is "powerful beyond measure." Nicole was moving from "gold-level" giving to "platinum-level" giving. Here's the gold-level version:

- Nicole gives money and her time to Room to Read.
- This is a great thing to do.
- It benefits her and it benefits the organization.

We love the gold-level version—it's fantastic! Please don't misinterpret our point here—this alone is certainly enough. However, this is also exactly the point at which we can all go further, and where Nicole is already going.

Here's the platinum-level version of giving:

• Nicole gives money and her time to Room to Read.
• This is a great thing to do.
• It benefits her and it benefits the organization.
• Nicole is now beginning to intentionally connect the dots between her donations of money and time and the ability of those donations to truly make an impact in the lives of countless others and to make a difference in the world.
• This energizes her.
• This energy is beginning to shift her own perception of her role and her impact in the world. She may not know the details or the full extent of this role, but she's sure it extends well beyond New Jersey, and she wants very much to discover more about it.
• This perceptual shift continues to energize and excite her, causing her to continue to give, to see even more possibilities, to do even more good, and to encourage other people to do the same. Some of these people may end up doing the same thing she is. It becomes a wonderful, powerful feedback loop. Nicole is at her financial summit and she sees nothing but blue skies and possibility ahead. This is Nicole's light!

If we go back to the Williamson quote now, Nicole really did seem a little frightened of it, a little reluctant to make such a big claim about herself. That's understandable. Yet she *is* changing the world through her work with Room to Read. It's a big thing to say, and an even bigger thing to do!

How Will You Shine?

Now, we *are* talking about big stuff here. The biggest. It just doesn't get any more significant than fighting to establish peace, relieve global poverty, advance education, or participate in any of the myriad initiatives under way to make the world a better place. Some of you are actively engaged in these kinds of initiatives right now, and to you we offer our deepest encouragement and gratitude. For most of us, though, "saving the world," as the Dalai Lama suggested we might do, or even changing it, as Nicole in New Jersey has set her sights on, is overwhelming. It's easily viewed at best as an idealistic notion and at worst as something completely beyond reach. If you're thinking something along the lines of "I've got three kids, two jobs, and a terrier—I don't have time to change the world," we get it.

But there is a different way of looking at it. If changing the world seems implausible, think about the light you can shine and the impact you can have and may already have within your own city, neighborhood, or living room. What could your actions lead to? What effects are they having now and what might they have in the future? If you extrapolate just a little, it gets really exciting, really fast. In workshops, people have created Prosperity Pictures that include images with all sorts of "shine" implications. Nineteen-year-old Yvonne is putting herself through college, working part-time, and struggling to make ends meet. She has a family photo in her "Sooner/More Money" box that, to her, represents her mother. She explained that her mom is in poor health and doesn't have much money, so Yvonne is planning to take care of her, probably in the not too distant future. At the tender age of nineteen, she doesn't quite know yet how she'll do it, but she's starting to think it through.

Would she characterize her intentions as "changing the world"? Probably not. Would we? Absolutely! It takes a special person to take on that kind of responsibility at any age, let alone at nineteen. What impact will Yvonne's actions have on her mom, on her extended family, on friends who see firsthand what she's doing? What might she inspire in others? What kinds of decisions will she make when she's twenty-nine or thirty-nine, given her altruism this early in life? The possibilities are endless.

Monaica runs a successful marketing business and will work only with clients who are open to including charitable giving as part of their marketing strategy. Many of these clients hadn't thought about deliberately giving to charity before they began their work with Monaica. They quickly realize that Monaica's advice will help them do well in their business by doing good in the world. Meg, the same woman from Chapter One who wants to go on an African safari, has the volunteer image in her "Sooner/More Money" box. In creating her Prosperity Picture, she realized that donating more money to charity is a priority for her. She has been buying tickets to charity events here and there as a way of giving back, but decided she wanted to do more, and has now revised her spending plan to save more money to donate. Who knows how Meg's generosity might affect others or how the beneficiaries of her increased charitable contributions might pay it forward.

Compared with something like fighting global hunger on another continent, these individual acts may at first seem rather modest, but every kind and generous act makes an impact. Monaica, Yvonne, Meg, and countless others like them are in fact making the world better, one small corner at a time. Imagine each act of generosity as a piece of an enormous jigsaw puzzle of the earth. Alone one piece might not seem like much, but when many pieces are put together an image of a beautiful planet begins to appear. The more people who make decisions with a broader impact in mind, and the more often they make them, the more impact they'll have. And the more the world will benefit.

Maureen, a wife, mother, and professional in metro Chicago is another great example of someone who's working on her personal way to shine. She has the picture of the family on her Prosperity Picture. For her, this photo represents her goal of doing volunteer counseling with couples who want to adopt children via open adoption, a method that allows an adopted child's birth parents to maintain contact with their biological child over time. Maureen and her husband Jonathon adopted their own energetic little boy Robby four years ago in an open adoption. It's a wonderful concept, but also one that can be emotional and scary for all involved. It took years of effort, a great deal of money and research, and a lot of emotional ups and downs to navigate their open adoption of Robby. One of the unanticipated outcomes of this incredible experience for Maureen has been that she realizes she has a huge desire to be an advocate for other parents and children so that they can find one another and do the same thing. She's looking into ways that she can both informally and formally help others walk through the complex process. This is Maureen's light—it's her way to shine. As she helps these adoptive parents, birth parents, and children, think of the impact she'll have not just on their lives, but also on the lives of the people in their immediate circles, and then that group's circles, and so on.

Become an Abundance Activist®

If you like this idea of intentionally cultivating prosperity for yourself and others, consider becoming an Abundance Activist. Abundance Activists are people who choose to see opportunities, optimism, and gratitude as a way not only to live their lives more prosperously, but also to make a positive difference for everyone they come in contact with. The idea for Abundance Activism came to Ellen during the Great Recession, when most people she met were focusing their attention on how bad things were in the economy. They were worried about their futures, substantially reducing their charitable contributions, and making lots of fear-based financial decisions. She saw stress and concern on the face of almost everyone she met.

Ellen knew that to get out of a difficult situation it's important to focus on what you want to happen, not what you are scared is going to happen. So, in each of her interactions, she tried to have the person leave feeling a little better, a little lighter, a bit more optimistic. To remind her to do this every time she spoke with someone, she wore a wristband with "Abundance Activist" written on it, and each time she completed a kind act, she would move the band to the other wrist. Her goal was to see how many times a day she could shift the band. Not only did this support Ellen in her giving focus, but it also made a difference for the recipients of her acts.

And then a funny thing happened. As Ellen focused her attention every day on being an Abundance Activist, her business began to grow. Even during a horrific economic crisis, business kept coming in. It was hard to explain, since many of her peers were cutting staff and seeing their incomes plummet during this same time. This is the yummy frosting on the prosperity cake—the more you give, the more you may see coming back your way.

Ellen calculated that if she told a hundred people about this idea and they decided to join in and share the notion, and within a day told two more people, and those two did the same, within about two weeks there would be more than 3.3 million Abundance Activists. That's a lot of good happening! Are you tired of bad news traveling fast and excited about the idea of good news spreading like wildfire? Then join us in becoming an Abundance Activist!

Abundance Activists realize they're part of a bigger whole, and that they have the ability to shift conversations from scarcity to abundance. Abundance Activists perpetuate love and generosity and refuse to give their time and attention to criticism, gossip, and "I win/you lose" thinking. They are awake to the truth that they are in control and responsible for how they react to life's challenges and opportunities—including financial challenges. They believe one of the best ways to grow their own prosperity is through focusing on serving others. Abundance Activists use money as a force for good in their world. We can all be Abundance Activists. Give it a try and track your progress by recording your Abundance Activist moments in your Prosperity Notebook, or by switching a wristband or bracelet from one arm to the other every time you complete a kind act.

Putting It All Together

What inspired us to write this book, and what encourages us when we lead workshops, is the chance to provide a financial framework for people to use so they can live extraordinary lives. So let's go a bit deeper and talk about how you can use the information in this book to make your life as extraordinary as it can be, taking

Maureen and her adoption advocacy as an example. Maureen has already completed Step One. She's created her Prosperity Picture, done her visualization, and is actively imprinting her adoption advocacy idea in her brain on a daily basis because she knows she needs her RAS to continually look for ways to make it happen, even when she isn't consciously thinking about it.

Practically speaking, she works full-time and is a wife and mother, so she doesn't have much time available to pursue advocacy work. One way to change that would be to build up enough savings so she could scale back her day job to a part-time paid position. Maureen can use Step Two to help her get super clear on what she owns and owes and what she spends. This information will be invaluable for her to plan how to responsibly make a change in her full-time position. Using Step Three, Maureen can begin to plan out how to make her career and advocacy dream combine into a financially responsible reality. She can work with her financial advisor to make smart decisions on how to invest her money to not only reach her immediate goals, but also make sure her longer-term investments are allocated wisely.

After Maureen gets her Prosperity Picture plan in place, she'll want to make sure she can actually get there. Step Four can help her with some inside work on her thoughts about this career transition to believe it is actually possible. When discouraging thoughts like "I can't possibly leave my job and still send Robby to college" come up, she can plan to say, "cancel/clear!" To build support, Maureen can meet with her financial advisor to plan out how her Prosperity priorities could be met if she scaled back on her job. She can also elicit the encouragement from a couple of girlfriends who are committed to seeing their friend Maureen live out her passion.

This path will quite possibly be financially challenging for Maureen. She'll use tools she's learned in Step Five to keep her spirits buoyed. And she is already laying the groundwork to keep her financial resilience strong using the suggestions in Step Six.

She has all the tools to get to her dream. But wait—there's just one more thing to think about. She's talking about impacting people's lives in major ways here and that's a scary thought. If she does this, she'll be in the thick of heart-wrenching moments: mothers giving up babies, or potentially not. Children having a chance at life opportunities that might not otherwise ever be available to them. Or not. Adoptive parents having their dreams come true. Or not. The chance to create an open, healthy dialogue among all those parties that will sustain them all moving forward. Or not. To go back to Marianne Williamson's quote, this really is power beyond measure. It is a chance to shine. And yes, it is scary. But once you have a glimpse of making a difference, and are doing what you are guided to do, turning back and ignoring that impulse becomes scary as well. So why not become an Abundance Activist? To Maureen, we say this: It may be uncomfortable to take this step forward, but you have the chance to benefit so many people, including yourself, that doing nothing may be equally as uncomfortable with no benefit on the horizon. *Use your power.*

And to you we say the same thing. Use your power and shine, whatever that means to you. The awe-inspiring Maya Angelou once famously said, "When you learn, teach; when you get, give." This book contains lots of tools to help you do that, but the real tools lie within you. What is your light? How will you shine? How are you powerful beyond measure? Those are big questions to answer, to be sure—much bigger than the scope of this book. But we are willing to bet that at least part of the answer to those questions is contained within your Prosperity Picture at this very moment. Is it nearby? Take a minute now to look at it again, or at least recall some of the images on your picture. Which ones say something about the unique ways that you shine, suggest ways that you want to provide light now or in the future? Pull out your Prosperity Notebook and answer this question: What contribution does my world need from me now?

Prosperity for a Lifetime

As you near the end of this book, you have a choice to make. You could take a moment to enjoy the satisfaction of having finished, and then proceed immediately to your bookshelf to file it between *How to Lose Twenty Pounds* and *How to Become Superwoman*, to be forgotten along with other ideas that, though attractive, you're not sure you have the time or energy to put into action. Or you could take a more proactive approach—do a quick mental review, identify a few key takeaways for yourself, and move ahead with putting these ideas into play as life and time allow. That, of course, would be better.

Or you could go farther. You could use this moment to decide you will really do something different in your life. This is the choice we hope you make, and it's also our greatest wish for you. We really, truly want you to put these concepts to work for yourself as you move forward. We know they can make a huge positive difference in your life, and we love that! And as we've discussed, there's more—the extra prize in the box of Cracker Jacks. If you work through these steps, make these concepts part of your regular routine, and continue to focus on your Prosperity Picture and what it means to you, you will create the potential not just to impact your own life positively, but to have a huge impact on the lives of people around you. And that's our biggest wish.

We know you have incredible abilities within you. We know you have light to shine that can make an impact well beyond the scope of our understanding and imagination. And we hope you are motivated right now to get out there and go for it! If you've been working through the prior chapters using the Prosperity Picture you've created and tackling the action items you've identified, you are ready to use your money as a force for good in the world. We also know you are human, you are busy, and you have multiple desires and demands that, at some point, will almost certainly get in the way of moving forward with these plans. What follows is designed to give you some strategies to use at such moments.

Keep Your Vision in Sight

In Chapter One we asked you to hang your Prosperity Picture up where you can see it every day. Is it set up in its spot right now? If it isn't, please put this book down, go get it, and hang it up. Why do we believe this is so important? Because we know that if you see these images on a regular basis and pay attention to them, they will work on your brain's RAS, continue to imprint, and you will begin to see desired results appear in your life quite possibly beyond what you even imagined. But if your Prosperity Picture is on the shelf in your closet under a stack of sweaters and you never see it, or if you only look at it a few times a year, you won't be taking this small and easy step that can yield such big results.

Refine Your Action Plan

We suggested you create an Action Plan for yourself in Chapter Two and a Goals List in Chapter Three. If you did this, you're already ahead of the game because these can serve as your basis for what you want to do moving forward. If you've created these items, find them in your Prosperity Notebook and take a few minutes to review them. What needs to be modified or added? Scan your Prosperity Picture and skim through the other chapters to see whether anything pops out that you want to add. Have any of your goals morphed or changed since you originally created your Prosperity Picture? Are you inspired by the notion of increasing not only your affluence but also your influence? If so, do you want to add an image or a goal to set you on the path to a big result? Have you come across a new image that's begging to be added to your Picture? Your Prosperity Picture is dynamic—you should plan to add to and change it over time to reflect your evolving vision of prosperity.

Haven't started your Action Plan or Goals List yet? No worries. Grab your Prosperity Notebook and create them now. Add as many items, big or small, as you would like. Your Action Plan could range from "Check car insurance premium" or "Call attorney to initiate estate plan" to "Look for higher-paying job," "Take a look at my 401(k) investment allocations," or "Give 50 percent more to my favorite philanthropic cause this year." Your Goals List can connect with any of the images on your Prosperity Picture. Make them as comprehensive as possible. But remember that they too, of course, will evolve over time. Make a commitment to yourself to review and update them a minimum of twice a year and a maximum of once a month, and write those review dates in your calendar. Your list will change and adapt over time as you accomplish certain goals and set new ones.

Use Your Calendar as a Tool

Speaking of calendars, they're another great tool to help you accomplish your action items and goals. If one of your action items is to finish your estate plan and you would like to have it done by October 1, record that date in your calendar. If, like Mary in Chapter Three, you have a goal of owning your home within three years, write that date down on a forward calendar. Note mini milestones in your calendar as well. For example, mark your goal of having one third of the money for your new house saved on a specific date each year for the next three years. These simple acts will create momentum and help keep you focused. Even if you don't quite make the goal by the anticipated date, this will serve as a reminder.

Make Prosperity a Habit

Does your Action Plan feel a bit overwhelming? You don't have to tackle all of your items at once and complete them by tomorrow. That said, we'd hate for you to be like the multitude of people who go for years avoiding many of the concepts and tasks in this book. We encourage you to think of prosperity as a habit to implement in your life. Just as you might have a habit of exercising three times a week, beginning each morning with a cup of coffee and a review of your day's plans, or enjoying a big family meal on Sundays, make a commitment to yourself to make prosperity a habit. As you do so, take a cue from Ian Newby-Clark at the University of Guelph in Ontario, Canada, who, in his research on habit change, has found that if people focus on changing more than one habit at a time, they risk becoming overloaded and changing none. So pick a starting point for your prosperity habit and work on one thing at a time.

When that's done, or at a natural pause point, go back to your list and pick a second item. Then repeat and continue. One at a time and all in good time.

Devote Extra Time to Bigger Prosperity Projects

Some of the smaller tasks on your list, like making phone calls or checking information, will be easy enough to accomplish quickly. But for bigger projects and ideas, it's helpful to break things down. Let's say one of your action items is to begin a regular practice of yoga and meditation to reduce your stress around money. Go to a fresh sheet in your Prosperity Notebook and write yourself a plan for doing this. When exactly will you fit this new activity into your day? Be realistic. Maybe you would like to incorporate thirty minutes of yoga and meditation into your morning seven days a week, but given the other demands on your time, can you really do that? Newby-Clark asserts that most people's plans are way too optimistic—they assume, in the execution of a new plan, that everything will turn out as well as it possibly can. So their "realistic" plan for a new exercise program ends up being virtually identical to their "best-case scenario" plan. As we all know, life brings unexpected events and things don't always happen in ways we expect. So to avoid disappointing yourself, build some flexibility into your plan.

Research also shows that creating "mini plans" is a powerful way to accomplish what you set out to do. These are the day-to-day details that make your plans sink or swim. Let's go back to your thirty-minute morning yoga/meditation plan. If you want to begin tomorrow morning, take a minute or two to "mini plan" tonight. You could tell yourself, "I will set the alarm thirty minutes earlier—for six thirty instead of seven. I know I'll be tired, so I'll have a cup of green tea and some fresh fruit to energize myself before I begin. I'll put the tea bags out tonight." It's a simple thing to do that can move your new initiative from possible to probable.

Set Up a Prosperity Circle®

As we talked about in Chapter Four, creating a solid support system is a terrific way to make your prosperity goals happen. Book clubs, cooking groups, money or investing clubs, and the like are a great way to pursue your goals with like-minded friends who share your interests. Why not start your own Prosperity Circle? Use this book as your guide and pick a particular chapter or topic to discuss at each meeting. You could also identify any of the activities or action steps and work on them with your Circle collaboratively. You can create your Prosperity Pictures together, do the visualization exercises as a group, organize a stress-reducing yoga or meditation evening, pool your giving for greater impact, and even bounce ideas off one another on more tactical issues such as creating an optimal spending plan or tips on getting the best insurance deals. If your Prosperity Circle members like formal accountability, share your prosperity goals with one another and then check in on the progress you've each made. You can make this group as formal or informal as you want, but we do suggest setting a regular meeting schedule (once a month is common), aiming for a Circle size between eight and twelve, and designating one person at each meeting to identify the specific topic for that day and to facilitate the conversation. See PictureYourProsperity.com for more details and ideas.

Not a Group Person? Find a Prosperity Partner

If making prosperity a group activity doesn't feel right to you, how about finding one person to team up with? We've repeatedly stressed the importance of having a support team, and this is just a way of formalizing that concept a bit more. Just as having a workout buddy motivates people to show up at the gym or hit the jogging path when they don't necessarily feel like it, establishing a designated Prosperity Partner can motivate you to maintain focus on the action steps and activities you've identified as most important. Your Prosperity Partner could be your significant other, a friend, or a family member—anyone, really, as long as you're both sincerely committed to pursuing the ideas and concepts we've discussed in this book and you both genuinely want to see the other person reach his or her goals. With your Prosperity Partner, you'll have an opportunity to check in regularly and hold each other accountable.

Keep Us in the Loop!

We absolutely love hearing people's stories of pursuing prosperity, so please keep us in the loop. Visit PictureYourProsperity.com and shoot us an e-mail about what you're focusing on and how it's going. What does your Prosperity Picture look like? What kinds of financial planning decisions are you making? What's working? How are you making a difference? Please share your success stories of abundance finding you. The more you pay attention to prosperity flowing your way, the more you will see all the riches already around you.

The End?

In a moment you will be done with this book. And what you do next will become the only thing that matters for your prosperity. For this reason, we don't think of this as the end, but instead the beginning!

Think back to that first visualization exercise in Chapter One, where you put yourself into one of your favorite images and thought about what you saw, heard, and felt. Do you want to see this actually happen in your life? Look at your Prosperity Picture and recall what some of the images represent. Would you like to see those become a reality? Think about your personal areas of dissatisfaction from Chapter Two. Do you want to see those change? How about the money moves that got you thinking in Chapter Three? Would you like to create a new investment plan or enhance an existing one that can help you push your vision into reality? What intrigued you in Chapter Four about the tactical ways you can make all these things happen for yourself? Want to be happy, relaxed, and resilient when it comes to managing your money? What struck you in Chapters Five and Six as being helpful to you personally for doing that? And as we discussed ways in this chapter that you could use your Prosperity Picture to influence the world beyond yourself, what came to mind? What light will you shine? How will you go even beyond your gold to a platinum level of contributing? All of these are ways to begin.

What will you do? What commitment can you make to yourself right now? What are you willing to do to make whatever is most important in these areas happen? Whatever you want, whatever you need, whatever you're thinking about right now, our wish for you is that you go out and do it. Make it happen!

And so we close with a quote that excites us and motivates us every time we hear it. In the words of the venerable and awe-inspiring Eleanor Roosevelt: "The future belongs to those who believe in the beauty of their dreams."

May you live a long, prosperous, light-filled life. One filled with lavish abundance. Here's to your beginning. Here's to your dreams!

Gain Traction Through Action

• Let your light shine. Review your Prosperity Picture and identify the images that have the potential to make an impact beyond yourself. Decide what you'll do to make them a reality.

• Become an Abundance Activist. Share your message of positivity and giving through your words and actions. Notice how you inspire others through your example. Track your kind acts by noting them in your Prosperity Notebook or by switching a wristband or bracelet with each kind act.

• Hang your Prosperity Picture if you haven't already done so.

• Review your Action Plan and Goals List. Do you need to make any revisions or additions? Make sure to review these regularly.

• Use your calendar to help make prosperity a habit. Note in your calendar when you will accomplish the actions in your plan.

• Create a support team around you. Set up times to meet with a Prosperity Circle or Prosperity Partner to support each other in continued learning, giving, and taking action toward achieving your plans.

• Keep us posted! Share your success stories with us by going to PictureYourProsperity.com.

ACKNOWLEDGMENTS— OUR PLATEFUL OF GRATEFUL

From Ellen and Lisa:

The birthing of *Picture Your Prosperity* was supported by so many supportive and enthusiastic people. We love having the ability to publically give them shout-outs here. Wouldn't it be cool if, at the end of any big project, not just for books, people wrote out their acknowledgments in an open forum?

To start, we are grateful for the input, guidance, and inspiration we received from so many attendees at the Your Prosperity Picture workshops as well as from the Invesco sales teams and financial advisors who sponsored these events. Your openness to share your personal stories, your Prosperity Pictures, and especially your enthusiasm fueled our writing.

A special thanks to all of the smart, inspirational people who agreed to be interviewed for *Picture Your Prosperity*. You *are* this book!

A huge thank you to our agent, Scott Hoffman—you opened the gateway for us! From the moment we met with you at the eyebrow raiser of a hotel bar and from each moment forward, you have been an incredible advocate and supporter. We are so lucky to work with you.

To Adrian Zackheim, Maria Gagliano, Will Weisser, and the entire team at Portfolio Penguin—we so appreciate your believing in this project. Your insight and expert guidance have been invaluable.

To Mike Collins and Lorri Ottis—thank you for your expert guidance in the areas of insurance and estate planning.

To Tracy Fielder and Charles Nix—thank you for your investment research assistance.

To Olivia Gauthier for your wonderful research and attention to details that made our eyes blurry.

The Prosperity Picture concept was made so much more powerful by the suggestions and input from Dave Saylor. Dave—your balloon drop is currently being organized!

From Ellen:

This book would not be what it is without the mentoring from Chris Attwood, Janet Bray Attwood, Marci Shimoff, and Geoff Affleck. I am so grateful for your expert guidance in all matters book related and even more grateful for your inspiration and encouragement to expand my view on what is possible and to step up and serve in a big way.

Thank you to Graham White for helping to formulate the big idea for women changing the world with their wealth. To Monaica Ledell—thank you for sticking with me to find ways to change lives for the better. I am so grateful to Denise Brown for the opportunity to share and clarify ideas with your Caregiving.com audience as well as for your solutions fund concept.

I so appreciate the weekly support from my mastermind team of Maggie Katz and Gina Calvano. And thank you to Phyllis Campagna for her ongoing love and support. Who would have ever thought a coaching relationship could last almost twenty years!

I am grateful every day for the gals in Northfield: Sandi Gore, Ann Adamson, and Susan Knight, for your support and flexibility. Boy, am I lucky to have you all on my team.

Sappy as this may sound, Lisa, I think the stars were aligned when Holly Danziger introduced us. From day one you have been a total joy to work with. You make me laugh and make writing really fun. You are totally rad and my lady-bro-sister.

And big hugs go out to my family. Every single day I think about how blessed I am to share my life with you. Amy and Benjy—you are the best. I am the luckiest mom around to have you two as kids. And to Steven—thank you for your heart, your love, your example of serving the world, and your being my partner in this journey of life.

From Lisa:

Albert Schweitzer was quoted as saying, "Each of us has cause to think with deep gratitude of those who have lighted the flame within us." For the flames lit within me, I would like to thank:

Ellen Rogin—you have been an incredible partner and inspiration! This collaboration has been nothing short of amazing.

Scott West, Gary Demoss, Gursh Kundan, and our entire team—thank you for your leadership, mentorship, and constant belief in me. I count my blessings with each passing year of working with each of you.

My Invesco Women's Network colleagues—I am grateful for your leadership, excited about our momentum, and motivated about what we can continue to accomplish together for women across the industry.

Mom—you really are my hero and my blessing. Thank you from the bottom of my heart.

Dad—thank you for always being exactly who you are, for always being there, and for making me laugh.

My amazing, beautiful friends and family—you know who you are! You inspire me, and you make my heart sing and my life full each and every day.

PA—you, and your constant support and encouragement throughout this process, are truly a godsend!

Hannah and Jimmy—you are both excellent human beings and delightful kids and I am lucky to have you in my life. May we always share extra room for activities and bottomless jars of fancy sauce.

TG—I wouldn't be here now and I wouldn't be who I am without you. Thank you for believing in me, supporting me, and loving me. I thank God for you every day . . . and I am a very, very lucky girl!

NOTES

Introduction

Page

1 Merriam Webster defines "prosperity": *Merriam-Webster,* www.merriam
-webster.com/dictionary/prosperity.

3 women direct $20 trillion of purchases: Muhtar Kent, "This Century Goes to the
Women," *Huffington Post,* October 13, 2010, www.huffingtonpost.com/muhtar
-kent/post_1057_b_762044.html.

3 control more than half of the wealth: Judith E. Nichols, "Understanding the Increasing Affluence of Women," Supporting Advancement, www.supportingadvancement
.com/vendors/canadian_fundraiser/articles/womens_affluence.htm.

Chapter One
Step One: Create Your Personal Vision

13 Little Prince makes this observation: Antoine de Saint-Exupéry, *The Little Prince.*

16 "It is now a well-known fact": Srinivasan Pillay, "The Science of Visualization:
Maximizing Your Brain's Potential During the Recession," *Huffington Post,* March
3, 2009, www.huffingtonpost.com/srinivasan-pillay/the-science-of-visualizat
_b_171340.html.

16 four groups of Olympic athletes: Robert Scaglione and William Cummins,
Karate of Okinawa: Building Warrior Spirit with Gan, Soku, Tanden, Riki
(North Clarendon, VT: Tuttle, 1993).

17 U.S. Olympic Committee now has increased: Rebecca A. Clay, "Gold-Medal Psychology," *Monitor on Psychology,* American Psychological Association, July/August
2012, http://www.apa.org/monitor/2012/07-08/sports.aspx.

19 the reticular activating system: "Reticular Activating System: Neural Bases of
Behavior," http://psychology.jrank.org/human-behavior/pages/cmxyrsctao/reticular
-activating-system-neural-bases.html.

20 you can help set the filter on your RAS: John Assaref and Murray Smith, *The Answer: Grow Any Business, Achieve Financial Freedom, and Live an Extraordinary Life* (New York: Atria, 2008).

20 influence and maximize the benefits of our RAS: Srinivasan Pillay, "The Science of Visualization: Maximizing Your Brain's Potential During the Recession," *Huffington Post*, March 3, 2009, www.huffingtonpost.com/srinivasan-pillay/the-science-of-visualizat_b_171340.html.

26 subconscious mind is unable to discern: John Assaraf and Murray Smith, *The Answer*.

Chapter Two
Step Two: Take Charge of Your Financial Wellness

53 About one in five households: Frank Stafford, Bing Chen, and Robert Schoeni, "Mortgage Distress and Financial Liquidity: How U.S. Families Are Handling Savings, Mortgages and Other Debts," *Panel Study of Income Dynamics: Technical Paper Series*, May 2012, http://psidonline.isr.umich.edu/Publications/Papers/.

62 conflicts about money lead more couples to divorce: Jeffrey Dew, Sonya Britt, and Sandra Huston, "Examining the Relationship Between Financial Issues and Divorce," *Family Relations* 61, no. 4 (2012): 615–28.

66 Americans don't have an estate plan: "Majority of American Adults Remain Without Wills," Lawyers.com, April 3, 2007, http://press-room.lawyers.com/majority-of-american-adults-remain-without-wills.html.

Chapter Three
Step Three: Design a Winning Plan

92 average annual return of the S&P 500: "CAGR of the Stock Market: Annualized Returns of the S&P 500," Moneychimp, www.moneychimp.com/features/.

97 the majority of the windows remained intact: Tracy Fielder and Charles Nix, investment index research 2014.

107 Researchers conducted a study in which monkeys: Laurie Santos, "A Monkey Economy as Irrational as Ours," TED Talk, July 2010.

Chapter Four
Step Four: Make It Happen

124 the "nocebo effect": "The Nocebo Response," *Harvard Mental Health Letter,* May 2005, www.health.harvard.edu/newsweek/The_nocebo_response.htm.

124 In one experiment: http://www.ncbi.nlm.nih.gov/pubmed/17484949.

124 in an antidepressant drug trial one patient: Roy R. Reeves, Mark E. Ladner, Roy H. Hart, and Randy S. Burke, "Nocebo Effects with Antidepressant Clinical Drug Trial Placebos," *General Hospital Psychiatry* 29, no. 3 (2007): 275–77.

127 average number of thoughts we have per day: "Brain Trivia," Laboratory of Neuro Imaging, www.loni.usc.edu/about_loni/education/brain_trivia.php.

Chapter Five
Step Five: Boost Your Financial Happiness Quotient

159 you may actually end up feeling depressed: Lawrence M. Berger, J. Michael Collins, and Laura Cuesta, "Household Debt and Adult Depressive Symptoms," January 15, 2013, http://papers.ssrn.com/sol3/papers.cfm?abstract_id=2200927; "Damn Right, I've Got the Blues," Squared Away blog, Center for Retirement Research at Boston College, January 10, 2010, http://squaredawayblog.bc.edu /squared-away/research/%E2%80%9Cdamn-right-ive-got-the-blues%E2% 80%9D/.

161 improve overall well-being and happiness: "The Benefits of Gratitude," *Psychology Today,* www.psychologytoday.com/basics/gratitude.

161 boost your happiness levels more than doubling your income: Robert Emmons, "10 Ways to Become More Grateful," Greater Good, November 17, 2010, http://greatergood.berkeley.edu/article/item/ten_ways_to_become_more _grateful1/.

162 Gratitude can reduce materialism: Emily L. Polak and Michael E. McCullough, "Is Gratitude an Alternative to Materialism?," *Journal of Happiness Studies* 7, no. 3 (2006): 343–60.

162 materialism seems to *reduce* happiness: Martin E. P. Seligman, *Authentic Happiness: Using the New Positive Psychology to Realize Your Potential for Lasting Fulfillment* (New York: Free Press, 2002), 55.

163 likability factor helps make grateful people better managers: Michael E. McCullough, Shelley D. Kilpatrick, Robert A. Emmons, and David B. Larson, "Is Gratitude a Moral Affect?," *Psychological Bulletin* 127, no. 2 (2001): 249–66.

163 One study revealed that students: Jan-Emmanuel De Neve and Andrew J. Oswald, "Estimating the Influence of Life Satisfaction and Positive Affect on Later Income Using Sibling Fixed Effects," *Proceedings of the National Academy of Sciences* 109, no. 49 (December 4, 2012), www.pnas.org/content/109/49/19953.

163 people who are highly positive and have strong self-esteem: Michael Como, "Do Happier People Make More Money? An Empirical Study of the Effect of a Person's Happiness on Their Income," *Park Place Economist* 19, no. 1 (2011), http://digitalcommons.iwu.edu/parkplace/vol19/iss1/8.

164 More than half of all Americans have less: Angela Johnson, "76% of Americans Are Living Paycheck-to-Paycheck," CNNMoney, June 24, 2013, http://money.cnn.com/2013/06/24/pf/emergency-savings/.

165 after people reach about $75,000 of income: Daniel Kahneman and Angus Deaton, "High Income Improves Evaluation of Life But Not Emotional Well-Being," *Proceedings of the National Academy of Sciences* 107, no. 38 (September 21, 2010), www.pnas.org/content/107/38/16489.full.

166 it depends on how you use it: Francis J. Flynn, "Research: Can Money Buy Happiness?," Stanford Graduate School of Business, September 25, 2013, www.gsb.stanford.edu/news/headlines/research-can-money-buy-happiness; Elizabeth W. Dunn, Lara B. Aknin, and Michael I. Norton, "Spending Money on Others Promotes Happiness," *Science* 319, no. 5870 (March 21, 2008), www.sciencemag.org/content/319/5870/1687.abstract.

166 the word "philanthropy": *Merriam-Webster,* www.merriam-webster.com/dictionary/philanthropy.

166 88 percent of people who donate: "Charitable Giving Statistics," National Philanthropic Trust, www.nptrust.org/philanthropic-resources/charitable-giving-statistics/.

166 Estimates on charitable giving: "Charitable Giving in America: Some Facts and Figures," National Center for Charitable Statistics, http://nccs.urban.org/nccs/statistics/Charitable-Giving-in-America-Some-Facts-and-Figures.cfm; "How America Gives," *Chronicle of Philanthropy,* August 20, 2012, http://philanthropy.com/section/How-America-Gives/621?cid=megamenu.

170 government lets you deduct part or all: "Eight Tips for Deducting Charitable Contributions," IRS, March 22, 2011, www.irs.gov/uac/Eight-Tips-for-Deducting-Charitable-Contributions.

172 "generativity": Stephen Post and Jill Neimark, *Why Good Things Happen to Good People* (New York: Broadway Books, 2007).

172 Generativity in older adults helps protect: Morris A. Okun, Ellen W. Yeung, and Stephanie Brown, "Volunteering by Older Adults and Risk of Mortality: A Meta-Analysis," *Psychology and Aging* 28, no. 2 (June 28, 2013), www.ncbi .nlm.nih.gov/m/pubmed/23421326/?i=4&from=/23545605/related.

175 Brooks found in his research: Arthur C. Brooks, "Does Giving Make Us Prosperous?," *Journal of Economics and Finance* 31, no. 3 (Fall 2007): 403–11; Arthur C. Brooks, "Giving Makes You Rich," *Upstart Business Journal*, September 23, 2012, http://upstart.bizjournals.com/views/columns/2007/10/15/Charity -Makes-Wealth.html?page=all.

176 Giving is likely to make you feel happy: Arthur C. Brooks, "Why Giving Matters," *BYU Magazine*, Summer 2009, http://magazine.byu.edu/?act=view&a=2441.

176 donating to charity may also contribute to our bottom lines: Zoe Chance and Michael I. Norton, "I Give, Therefore I Have: Giving and Subjective Wealth," http://faculty.chicagobooth.edu/workshops/marketing/past/pdf/zoe%20chance .pdf; Kathleen Doheny, "Give Away Your Money, Feel Happier?," HealthDay, January 21, 2013, http://health.usnews.com/health-news/news/articles/2013 /01/21/give-away-your-money-feel-happier.

Chapter Six

Step Six: Become Financially Resilient

189 Mount Saint Helens: Andrea Thompson, "Mount St. Helens Still Recovering 30 Years Later," LiveScience, May 17, 2010, www.livescience.com/6450-mount-st -helens-recovering-30-years.html.

194 your respiratory system sends messages to your brain: Richard P. Brown and Patricia L. Gerbarg, *The Healing Power of the Breath: Simple Techniques to Reduce Stress and Anxiety, Enhance Concentration, and Balance Your Emotions* (Boston: Trumpeter, 2012).

194 Researchers also found that stress increases: M. Mather and N. R. Lighthall, "Risk and Reward Are Processed Differently in Decisions Made Under Stress," *Current Directions in Psychological Science* 21, no. 1 (2012): 36–41.

195 "scarcity directly reduces bandwidth": Sendhil Mullainathan and Eldar Sharif, *Scarcity: Why Having Too Little Means So Much* (London: Allen Lane, 2013).

196 *increase* creative thinking and problem-solving abilities: Lorenza S. Colzato, Ayca Ozturk, and Bernhard Hommel, "Meditate to Create: The Impact of

Focused-Attention and Open-Monitoring Training on Convergent and Divergent Thinking," *Frontiers in Psychology* 3 (2012); Viviana Capurso, Franco Fabbro, and Cristiano Crescentini, "Mindful Creativity: The Influence of Mindfulness Meditation on Creative Thinking," *Frontiers in Psychology* 4 (2013).

199 studies have found yoga to be effective: Amy Novotney, "Yoga as a Practice Tool," *Monitor on Psychology*, American Psychological Association, November 2009, www.apa.org/monitor/2009/11/yoga.aspx.

201 If you accrued $1 million thirty years ago: "Inflation Calculator: Bureau of Labor Statistics," U.S. Bureau of Labor Statistics, www.bls.gov/data/inflation_calculator.htm.

202 brains are actually wired to give priority to bad news: Daniel Kahneman, *Thinking, Fast and Slow* (New York: Farrar, Straus and Giroux, 2011).

202 ingested more financial news actually had lower investment returns: Bob Frick, "Overload of Information Can Be a Disadvantage to Investors," *Washington Post*, July 18, 2010, www.washingtonpost.com/wp-dyn/content/article/2010/07/16/AR2010071606797.html.

219 two thirds of initial claims are denied: "Disabled-Worker Statistics," Social Security Administration, www.ssa.gov/oact/STATS/dibStat.html; "Disability Statistics," Council for Disability Awareness, www.disabilitycanhappen.org/chances_disability/disability_stats.asp.

Chapter Seven
Step Seven: Build a Lifetime of Prosperity

228 "The world will be saved": Linda Lowen, "The Dalai Lama: 'The World Will Be Saved by the Western Woman,'" Women's Issues, About.com, October 19, 2009, http://womensissues.about.com/b/2009/10/19/the-dalai-lama-the-world-will-be-saved-by-the-western-woman.htm.

229 "naturally compassionate": Victor Chan, "Western Women Can Come to the Rescue of the World," Dalai Lama Center, January 25, 2010, http://dalailama center.org/blog-post/western-women-can-come-rescue-world.

229 evidence that women business owners across the globe: Candida Brush, "How Women Entrepreneurs Are Transforming Economies and Communities," *Forbes*, February 16, 2013, www.forbes.com/sites/babson/2013/02/16/how-women-entrepreneurs-are-transforming-economies-and-communities/.

229 "There's a growing recognition among everyone": Nicholas D. Kristof and Sheryl WuDunn, "The Women's Crusade," *New York Times*, August 22, 2009,

www.nytimes.com/2009/08/23/magazine/23Women-t.html?pagewanted=
all&_r=0.

229 estimated that as much as $59 trillion: Paul G. Schervish and John J. Havens,
"New Report Predicts U.S. Wealth Transfer of $59 Trillion, with $6.3 Trillion in
Charitable Bequests, from 2007–2061," Center on Wealth and Philanthropy, Boston
College, May 28, 2014, www.bc.edu/content/dam/files/research_sites/cwp/pdf
/Wealth%20Press%20Release%205.28-9.pdf.

229 70 percent of that money will end up: Kristan Wojnar and Chuck Meek, "Women's
Views of Wealth and the Planning Process," Advisor Perspectives, March 1, 2011,
www.advisorperspectives.com/newsletters11/Womens_Views_of_Wealth_and
_the_Planning_Process.php.

230 How much is $25 trillion?: "How Big Is a Trillion?," BobKrumm.com, February
12, 2009, www.bobkrumm.com/blog/2009/02/how-big-is-a-trillion/.

230 For a start, every child on the planet: Paul Glewwe, Meng Zhao, and Melissa
Binder, *Achieving Universal Basic and Secondary Education: How Much Will
It Cost?* (Cambridge, MA: American Academy of Arts and Sciences, 2006); Leen
Abdallah, "Cost to End World Hunger," Borgen Project, February 15, 2013,
http://borgenproject.org/the-cost-to-end-world-hunger.

246 research on habit change: Ian Newby-Clark, "Five Things You Need to Know
About Effective Habit Change," Zen Habits, November 5, 2007, http://zenhabits
.net/five-things-you-need-to-know-about-effective-habit-change/.

INDEX

Abundance Activist, 239–40

abundance effect, 125–26

accountability, 185

accounts, streamlining of, 207

Action Plan for financial wellness, 59–66
asset allocation and, 59–60
communicating with spouse about
money and, 62–63
insurance and, 64–65
refining, 245
saving and investing right amount for
yourself and, 60–62
will/estate planning and, 65–66

advisors, financial. *See* professional
financial advisors

affluence, growing of by giving, 175–76

Angelou, Maya, 242

Apple, 95

asset allocation. *See* diversification

assets, inventory of, 47–53, 69–71

athletes, and visualization, 16–17

auto insurance, 217

automatic savings plans, 130

balance, 199–200

Bank, Grameen, 229

Barclays Capital U.S. Aggregate Index, 96

Barrons.com, 109

behavioral finance, 129–30

beliefs, financial. *See* financial beliefs

beneficiaries, 222

Berger, Lawrence, 159

beta, 125

bill-paying system, 207

Biology of Belief, The (Lipton), 120

bond funds, 89

bonds, 89, 96

brain training, 20–22

breathing, 193–95

Brooks, Arthur, 175

budget. *See* spending plan

cancel/clear technique, 127

cash reserves, 132

certificates of deposit (CDs), 89

Certified Financial Planner
(www.letsmakeaplan.org), 151

Chaponot, Tamara, 5–9, 77

charitable organizations, 170

childbirth, and visualization, 17

children, designating legal guardians and
trustees for, 222–24

Clever Alice, 6, 7, 8, 77

clutter, clearing, 203–7
accounts, streamlining of, 207
bill-paying system, establishing, 207
documents, listing and ordering of,
205–6
filing system for paperwork, setting
up, 206–7

clutter, clearing (*cont.*)
home, inventory of, 205
mental, 204
physical, 204
safe-deposit box, use of, 205
college flowerpot, 137–38
college savings plans, 137–38
commodity stocks, 96
compound interest, 84–88
contingent beneficiaries, 222
corporate trustees, 223
couples, 147–50
communications about money and,
62–63, 147
financial basics, understanding, 148–49
foundational financial building blocks
for, 149–50
joint Prosperity Picture, developing,
39–42
Couples Prosperity Picture, 41–42
creativity, 189–92
credit card debt, 49–53
minimum payment trap and,
50–53
stress and, 159–60

Dalai Lama, 228–29, 236
debt reduction, and financial happiness,
159–61
disability insurance, 219
diversification, 59–60, 97–99
style, 93–94
theory behind, 97–99
documents
financial documents, list of key, 153–55
inventory of, 205–6
downturns. *See* financial downturns,
weathering
dry needling, 17
durable power of attorney, 221–22

economic downturns. *See* financial
downturns, weathering
Edgar, Stacey, 167–68
emergency fund. *See* solutions flowerpot
employer-sponsored retirement plans,
134–35
equity line of credit, 132–33
essential matters, 13–15
estate planning, 65–66, 220–24
beneficiaries, 222
children and, 222–24
durable power of attorney, 221–22
revocable living trusts, 221
wills, 221

figures versus essential matters, 13–15
filing system for paperwork, 206–7
financial advisors. *See* professional
financial advisors
financial beliefs, 113–55
action steps, summary of, 150–52
confidence and expansiveness, steps
for moving to, 126–28
development of, in childhood, 120–21
financial documents, list of key, 153–55
financial flowerpot system and, 129–39
inner money beliefs, understanding,
115–20
negative thinking, consequences of,
123–26
prioritizing goals and, 128–29
professional financial advisor, hiring,
142–46
savings percentages and, 139–40
self-exploration of, 122–23
spouse/significant other, working
with, 147–50
supportive mind-set, importance of,
113–20
support team, building, 141–42

financial creativity, 189–92

financial documents, list of key, 153–55

financial downturns, weathering, 207–20
 cyclical nature of markets, 207–8
 financial fears, dealing with, 211–14
 insurance and, 216–20
 spending plan, adding values
  component to, 210–11
 support team, leaning on, 214–16
 Truth Talk technique for dealing with
  financial fears, 211–14

financial flowerpot system, 129–39
 automatic savings plans and, 130
 college flowerpot, 137–38
 example of, 138–39
 investment types should be matched
  to timing of goals, 130–31
 retirement flowerpot, 133–38
 solutions flowerpot, 131–33

financial happiness, 9–10, 157–82
 action steps, summary of, 181–82
 debt reduction and, 159–61
 giving and, 158, 167–77
 gratitude and, 158, 161–65
 money and, 165–66
 philanthropy and, 166
 stress reduction and, 158–61

financial information overload, stopping,
 202–3

financial plan
 action steps, summary of, 110
 compound interest and, 84–88
 diversification and (See diversification)
 example of intentional approach to,
  81–84
 investment categories, 94–99
 investment portfolio, building,
  99–110, 111
 long-term financial goals, investment
  options for, 90–99

moving Prosperity Picture ideas to
 reality, 78–80
 prioritizing goals, 80
 purchasing investment product, 110
 reality check for (See financial wellness)
 risk tolerance and, 106–9
 short-term financial goals, investment
  options for, 88–90
 visual element of (See Prosperity
  Picture)

Financial Planning Association
 (www.plannersearch.org), 151

financial resiliency, 9–10, 183–226
 accountability and, 185
 action steps, summary of, 225–26
 clutter, clearing, 203–7
 downturns, weathering, 207–20
 estate planning and, 220–24
 financial information overload,
  stopping, 202–3
 "I'll be okay" as baseline belief and,
  200–202
 living in prosperity versus frightened
  state of mind, 183–86
 perspective and, 186–92
 self-calming skills, building, 192–200

financial wellness, 9, 46–76
 Action Plan for, 59–66
 action steps, summary of, 67–68
 asset allocation to help meet goals
  and, 59–60
 communicating with spouse about
  money and, 62–63
 credit card debt, reviewing, 49–53
 determining what you have and what
  you owe, 46–55
 insurance and, 64–65
 inventory of assets and liabilities,
  47–53, 69–71
 net worth calculation, 53–55

financial wellness (*cont.*)
    quiz for, 56–59
    saving and investing right amount for
        yourself and, 60–62
    spending plan, creating, 53–55,
        71–76
    will/estate planning and, 65–66
FINRA BrokerCheck, 146
529 college savings plans, 105,
    137–38
fixed income. *See* bonds
flowerpot system. *See* financial
    flowerpot system
401(k) plans, 134–36
403(b) plans, 135
Frank, Anne, 230
Fried Green Tomatoes (movie), 64
FTSE NAREIT Equity REIT Index, 96

generativity, 171–72
giving, 8, 9, 158, 167–77, 231–40
    abundance activism and, 239–40
    account for, setting up, 168–69
    affluence and influence, giving to
        grow your, 175–76
    friends' causes, supporting, 167
    gold-level and platinum-level,
        234–35
    kind acts, doing, 174
    Prosperity Echo and, 231–32
    purchases, giving with, 167
    receiving and, 177–81
    retailers/products that give to
        charities, supporting, 167–68
    spending plan, as element of, 168
    tax benefits of, 170–71
    time and energy, giving of, 171–74
    volunteering, 174
giving account, 168–69
Global Girlfriend, 167–68

goals
    asset allocation to help meet, 59–60
    financial flowerpot system for
        attaining, 129–39
    moving goals to reality, 78–83
    organizing of, in Prosperity Picture,
        27–36
    prioritizing, 80, 128–29
    RAS conditioning and, 20–22
    refining, 245
gold-level giving, 234–35
Google, 95
gratitude, 8, 9, 158, 161–65
    benefits of, 162–64
    negative thinking, as means of
        pushing out, 164
    practice of, 161–62
    steps for incorporating gratitude into
        daily life, 164–65
growth stocks, 95
guardians, 222–23

happiness, financial. *See* financial happiness
*Happy Money: The Science of Smarter
    Spending* (Norton), 176
HealthCare.gov, 217
health insurance, 217
home, inventory of, 205
home equity line of credit, 132–33
home insurance, 217–18

"I'll be okay" baseline belief, 200–202
individual retirement accounts (IRAs), 136
influence, growing of by giving, 175–76
insurance, 64–65, 216–20
    auto, 217
    disability, 219
    health, 217
    home, 217–18
    inventory of, 220

life, 218–19
long-term care, 219–20
renter's, 218
umbrella, 218
international equities, 95–96
inventory
   of assets and liabilities, 47–53
   credit card debt, 49–53
   work sheet for, 69–71
   of home and documents, 205–6
   of insurance, 220
investment portfolio, building, 99–110
   Minivan Approach, 100, 101–2, 105, 108
   purchasing investment products, 110
   risk tolerance and, 106–9
   Sedan Approach, 100, 103–4, 108
   Sports Car Approach, 100, 104–5
IRS Publication 561, 171

Katie, Byron, 186–87
kind acts, 174
Kristof, Nicholas, 229

large cap stocks
   growth, 95
   value, 95
legal guardians, 222–23
liabilities
   credit card debt, 49–53
   inventory of, 47–53
   work sheet for, 69–71
life insurance, 218–19
lifetime prosperity, building, 227–51
   abundance activism and, 239–40
   action steps, summary of, 251
   calendar as tool to aid in, 246
   example of putting prosperity
      concepts to work, 240–43
   extra time for bigger projects,
      devoting, 247–48

gold- and platinum-level giving and,
   234–35
keeping your vision in sight, 244
making habit of prosperity, 246–47
personal "shine" and potential impacts
   of, 236–38
playing big and, 232–35
Prosperity Circle, setting up, 248
Prosperity Echo and, 231–32
Prosperity Partner, working with, 249
women as change makers, 228–31
likability, and gratitude, 163
Lipton, Bruce, 120
Little Prince, The (Saint-Exupéry), 13–14
long-term care insurance, 219–20
long-term financial goals, investment
   options for, 90–99
   commodity stocks, 96
   fixed income, 96
   international equities, 95–96
   large cap stocks, 95
   mid cap stocks, 95
   mutual funds, 91–92
   real estate stocks, 96
   small cap stocks, 94–95
   S&P 500 Index average annual
      returns, 92–93
   stocks, defined, 91
   style diversification and, 93–94
Lucky, 6

Maguire, Mairead Corrigan, 228–29
mantra, 198
materialism, 162
medical situations, and visualization, 17–18
meditation, 195–99
mental clutter, 204
Microsoft, 95
mid cap stocks, 95
mini-plans, 247–48

Minivan Approach, to building
     investment portfolio, 100, 101–2,
     105, 108
MissingMoney.com, 225
money
     financial plan (*See* financial plan)
     happiness and, 165–66
     prosperity and, 1–2
     silo view of, 2
     as tool, 2
     visualization exercise for examining
          beliefs on, 122–23
money market accounts, 88–89
Morningstar.com, 109
MSCI EAFE Index, 95–96
Mullainathan, Sendhil, 195
mutual funds, 91–92

National Association of Insurance and
     Financial Advisors (www.naifa.org),
     152
National Association of Personal Financial
     Advisors (www.napfa.org), 152
negative thinking, consequences of,
     123–26
Neimark, Jill, 172
net worth calculation, 53–55
Newby-Clark, Ian, 246, 247
Newman's Own, 167
nocebo effect, 124
Norton, Michael, 176

One Million Degrees, 231–32

perspective, 186–92
     financial creativity and, 189–92
     finding upside in down situations,
          188–89
Phair, Liz, 6
philanthropy, 166

physical clutter, 204
Pillay, Srinivasan, 16
placebo effect, 123–24
platinum-level giving, 234–35
portfolio, building. *See* investment
     portfolio, building
Post, Stephen, 172
prepaid tuition plans, 137
prioritizing goals, 80, 128–29
products that give to charities,
     supporting, 167–68
professional financial advisors, 142–46
     compensation of, 144–45
     determining whether to hire, 142–44
     researching and hiring, 145–46
prosperity, 1–10
     defined, 1
     financial beliefs and, 113–55
     financial happiness and, 9–10, 157–82
     financial resiliency and, 9–10, 183–226
     financial wellness and, 9, 46–76
     giving and, 8, 9, 158, 167–77, 231–40
     gratitude and, 8, 9, 158, 161–65
     lifetime of, building, 227–51
     money and, 1–2
     visualization and, 7–8, 9, 11–43
Prosperity Circle, 248
Prosperity Echo, 231–32
Prosperity Partner, 249
Prosperity Picture, 13–43
     action steps, summary of, 42–43
     Couples Prosperity Picture, 41–42
     defined, 13
     figures versus essential matters, 13–15
     goals, organizing, 27–36
     joint picture for couples, developing,
          39–42
     keeping vision in sight to keep
          brain-imprinting process working,
          36–38, 244

meaning of, analyzing, 31–36
moving goals to reality, 78–83
Prosperity Picture frame, drawing and organizing goals in, 27–31
RAS conditioning and, 22–27
purchasing investment product, 110

rational emotive behavior therapy, 211
real estate investment trusts (REITs), 96
real estate stocks, 96
receiving, 177–81
being open to, 178–81
giving and receiving as mutually supporting, 177
recticular activating system (RAS), 19–27
conditioning of, to achieve goals, 20–22
filtering mechanism of, 19–20
Prosperity Picture and, 22–27
renter's insurance, 218
resiliency, financial. See financial resiliency
retailers that give to charities, supporting, 167–68
retirement flowerpot, 133–38
allocation of retirement savings, 134–35
amount of money needed in retirement, determining, 133–34
employer-sponsored retirement plans, contributions to, 134–36
future income you'll receive, determining, 134
IRAs, contributions to, 136
when you want to retire, determining, 133
A Return to Love (Williamson), 232–33
revocable living trusts, 221
risk tolerance, 106–9
Robinson, Mary, 228–29
Room to Read, 234, 235

Roosevelt, Eleanor, 251
Roth 401(k) plans, 135
Roth IRAs, 136
Russell, 94, 95
Russell 1000 Growth Index, 95
Russell 2000 Index, 94
Russell Midcap Index, 95

safe-deposit box, 205
Saint-Exupéry, Antoine de, 13
savings accounts, 88–89
savings plan, 60–62
scarcity, 195
scientific basis, for visualization, 15–16, 19–22
Sedan Approach, to building investment portfolio, 100, 103–4, 108
self-calming skills, 192–200
balance, cultivating, 199–200
breathing and, 193–95
meditation and, 195–99
yoga and, 195, 199
SEP IRAs, 136
Sesame Street (TV show), 115, 195
Shafir, Eldar, 195
short-term bond funds, 89–90
short-term financial goals, investment options for, 88–90
certificates of deposit (CDs), 89
money market accounts, 88–89
savings accounts, 88–89
short-term bond funds, 89–90
significant other, working with. See couples
SIMPLE IRAs, 136
small cap stocks, 94–95
solutions flowerpot, 131–33
cash reserves, determining amount of, 132
equity line of credit, using, 132–33
S&P 500 Index, 92–93

spending plan, 53–55
  giving as element of, 168
  prioritizing expenses based on values,
    54–55
  values component, adding, 210–11
  work sheet for, 71–76
S&P GSCI Index, 96
sports, and visualization, 16–17
Sports Car Approach, to building
  investment portfolio, 100, 104–6
spouse, working with. *See* couples
stock market, 91–94
  cyclical nature of, 207–8
  investment categories, 94–99
  S&P 500 Index as gauge of overall
    performance of, 92–93
  style diversification and, 93–94
stocks, 91
stress reduction
  financial happiness and, 158–61
  financial information overload,
    stopping, 202–3
  self-calming skills and, 192–200
style diversification, 93–94
subjective wealth, 176
support team
  building, 141–42
  leaning on, in tough times, 214–16
  Prosperity Circle, setting up, 248
  Prosperity Partner, working with, 249

tax benefits of giving, 170–71
Ten Thousand Villages, 167
Thaler, Richard, 202–3
time and energy, giving of, 171–72
Toms Shoes, 167
Trading Places (movie), 96
traditional IRAs, 136
trustees, 223
Truth Talk technique, 211–14

umbrella insurance, 218
Ursiny, Tim, 128, 211, 213

value stocks, 95
visualization, 7–8, 9, 11–43
  athletes and, 16–17
  daydreaming, as element of financial
    strategy, 11–13
  for feeling of knowing you'll be okay,
    201–2
  of formative financial beliefs,
    122–23
  medical situations and, 17–18
  Prosperity Picture, creating, 13–43
  RAS-stimulating exercise, 24–27
  scientific basis for, 15–16, 19–22
volunteer, 174

*Why Good Things Happen to
  Good People* (Post & Neimark),
  172
Williams, Betty, 228–29
Williams, Jody, 228–29
Williams, Serena, 120
Williamson, Marianne, 232–33
wills, 65–66, 221
women, 228–31
  compassion and, 229
  foreign aid directed to, 229
  money likely to be transferred to and
    controlled by, 229–30
  reinvestment by women business
    owners, 229
WuDunn, Sheryl, 229

yoga, 195, 199
*Your Brain and Business: The
  Neuroscience of Great Leaders*
  (Pillay), 16
Yunus, Muhammad, 229

Looking for Some Extra Tools to Help You Build a Prosperous Future?

If you loved the book, we would love to help you take your Prosperity Picture to the next level with these free bonuses. Go to Picture YourProsperity.com "Book Bonuses" Tab and type in the password "PYPNow" when prompted to access the following:

- Printable materials for additional Prosperity Picture boards: Get your significant other, close friends, or the whole family involved in creating a vision for prosperity!
- Checklist for creating and managing your own Prosperity Circle®: don't get bogged down in the details. Our step-by-step guide makes running your group a snap.

Interested in Bringing Ellen & Lisa in to Speak to Your Group?

We're passionate about taking the book's message out into the world. Face-to-face interaction makes the activities and ideas in *Picture Your Prosperity* even more impactful. We can work with you to create an exciting, interactive live presentation, where your audience will be able to:

- Create their own vision of prosperity
- Learn ideas on how to make it happen
- Design a personal plan of action
- Handle their money with more joy and less stress
- Explore what true prosperity looks like

Visit PictureYourProsperity.com for more information.

Would you Like to Learn More About Abundance?

If you would like to sharpen your focus on abundance, connect personally with Ellen, America's Abundance Activist®. You can learn more about her programs and get more free resources, such as:

- The Abundance-o-Meter Quiz—learn where you fall on the abundance/scarcity scale
- "Prosperity in a Minute" Video Series
- The Prosperity Flow Meditation available for download

Ellen is available for media appearances, keynote speeches, and workshops. Visit EllenRogin.com for more information.